Bend in the Road

Rose Howe

More books by Rose Howe:

The Long and Winding Road
(prequel to *Bend in the Road*)

The Redneck Englishwoman Strikes Again!

Reflections of a Redneck Englishwoman

Diary of a Redneck Englishwoman

AVAILABLE AT AMAZON.COM

ISBN: 9798772731550
Independently published

ACKNOWLEDGEMENTS

This book has been a journey for me. Doors that stubbornly refused to budge were opened wide, what lay behind them closely examined and then, with their hinges well oiled, closed with ease. I went to work on those doors with the help and support of so many people.

I would like to thank my family. My brothers Charlie, David and Tommy who over the years since we were reunited, have filled in so many blank spots in my life. Darrell's children, Terresa, Susan and Andy, who have accepted me for who I am and shown me much love.

This sequel to my early life story "The Long and Winding Road," could not have come to fruition without the amazing help and encouragement of my dear friend and editor Pat Hutson. From her enthusiasm for my writing, the gentle nudges to keep at it, her impeccable editing but, most of all, her faith in me that people would want to read my story, I thank her.

To all my followers out there who get up on a Sunday morning, eagerly awaiting my next blog story and impatiently waiting to read my next book, many thanks to you too. For it is you who are such a large part in continuing to fuel my passion for writing.

Most of all, I cannot thank enough my dearest husband, Darrell. He knows of my past trials and tribulations and has encouraged me to lay them bare. Holding me tight in his arms when painful memories of the past made tears run freely from my eyes and sobs wrack my body, he encouraged me to write on. After 34 years together our love today is stronger than ever. He is my rock.

MY DEDICATION...

To my dearest Darrell.

INTRODUCTION

Drip, drip, drip, drip. Awakening to the sound, I turn slightly in bed and listen to the rain dripping from the eaves, the tears correspondingly run silently down my face. From the frying pan into the fire, I think as I lie in bed a few more minutes. Married seven years and now it is all over. I am alone – well not totally alone, lying across the foot of the bed is my dear dog Jasper and old Tom Cat is by my pillow.

"I guess I should be thankful I have you two!" I say out loud. No, I am not totally alone. Ahead of me a new life awaits; so why do I feel so afraid? I can survive on my own. After all, when my father took me away from my mother when I was just a wee toddler, he left her destitute with three young boys to raise, and she managed. Surely, I can too?

Well, it does no good to just lie here and mope about things. A good cup of tea always makes the day look better.

Swinging my legs out of bed, the old cat yawns, stretches and a giant purr escapes him as he flexes his paws, claws kneading the counterpane. Jasper, a fine-looking Golden Retriever, lifts his head and begins to wag his feathery tail before jumping down to the floor to follow me down the rickety stairs to the little kitchen below. Another day begins. When the kettle has boiled and first cup of tea of the day made, I sit on an upturned box, and I cannot help looking back over the past few years.

"What a blunder I made of things!" I murmur to myself, always seeming to turn the blame inwards instead of on others. Yet now and again, slowly but surely, I allow myself to look at the past seven years and realize it takes two to tango. Yes, the healing process is beginning.

"I have a roof – of sorts – over my head, an old cat and you, Jasper." I say as I stroke his head. "My little Morris car, who might be a rather decrepit looking but very serviceable 1973 VW Super Beetle and, most of all, a job. What more could I ask for!"

After letting Jasper and old Tom Cat out the back door, as I return to my upturned box to drink my tea, I cannot help but think once again about my mum. How, I wonder, would she have handled things? I allow my mind to wander back, remembering my childhood, wondering how different a person I might have been had I grown up knowing my mother.

Born in England, I was raised from a very early age by my father, a very domineering man. We moved frequently from village to village; it was years before I came to learn the reason why. Eventually I discovered my mother had not died when I was born as I had been led to believe, but was alive and well in Canada. So as a young girl I had no desire to know her. In fact, I was in dread of this woman, someone, as my father told me so many times, who did not like me or want me.

Years later, I came to discover this was not true at all. I learned what this woman went through to try and find me after my father stole me from her after he had moved the entire family to Canada. How he said he was taking me for a walk, but instead drove to the airport where he absconded with me to England. My mother never gave up hope, never gave up trying to find me. Fate played quite a hard role in my life as I grew up away from my mother, and yet Fate eventually brought my brothers back into my life and through them, my mum. I learned how much she loved me.

Sitting on my box, my tea forgotten and cold, it comes to me that maybe there is more of her in me than I thought after all. She was strong and resourceful, kind and loving, held passionately to her beliefs and loved her Scottish traditions. Would my life have been different had I stayed with my mother? Maybe...I will never know...but I do know she has always watched over me and been there in spirit for me--and still is to this day.

"Yes, I can do this!" I tell myself as I get up to let Jasper and Tom Cat back inside. I head into the kitchen, put the kettle on for another cup of tea, ready to face whatever the days ahead may bring.

Chapter One.

Drip, drip, drip, yes, it is raining again. As I lay in bed, telling myself to get up, I try not to focus on the soggy six-mile bicycle ride ahead of me. Six miles through busy morning traffic in order to reach the house where I work on the more posh side of Vancouver, British Columbia. My father and I live in Burnaby, a suburb you might say of Vancouver, although Vancouver has grown so large that the there is little distinction between it and its neighbouring burgs. Maybe I should take the bus to work today. As soon as the thought crosses my mind, I dismiss it. As meager as the bus fare is it will cut into my allowance, the twenty-five dollars my father allots me per month out of my wage. Anything I spend from those twenty-five dollars must be accounted for and surely bus fare, when I have a perfectly serviceable bicycle, would be considered frivolous and wasteful. Besides, if I spend $10 when my next paycheque rolls around, I get $10 – not $25 – to bring me back up to my original $25. No, I will don a mac and brave the rain and traffic on two wheels this morning.

I am a nanny to a young lad by the name of Bruce. I never thought I would ever have such a job, but after leaving the Butcher Boy Meat plant, it seemed a better alternative than being a bank teller! Bruce was a handful and a half but after an initial stormy confrontation, a strong bond of friendship and respect grew between us. My job was quite simple; arrive before his mother – who was a doctor – and his father – who was a surgeon – headed off to work, normally around 8 o'clock in the morning. Keep Bruce out of trouble and entertained the entire day until his mother returned home from work between 5 or 6 o'clock of an evening. Pretty easy work for which I was getting paid a whopper sum of nine hundred dollars a month!

Bruce was a very different child. Extremely intelligent, very willful and opinionated, but like a young horse, was looking for guidance and a set of rules to live by. I certainly had rules! No swearing, no peeing on the conservatory music room carpet – yes, he did do that once and worse! – no temper tantrums and we would get along just fine. Climbing trees was allowed and encouraged which was something he had never been permitted to do before, and as much running and jumping and playing outside in the garden as he wanted. With some boundaries established as to what I would tolerate, we did indeed become grand pals. I sure would miss this little lad when I left, as one day I knew I would. Being a nanny for the rest of my life was not what I wanted to do I kept telling myself over and over again. These were the thoughts that were running through my mind as I slogged through the rain, up hills and down on my old bicycle, making my way to the Cleator's house on the far side of Vancouver. Maybe I should have taken the bus after all.

As it turns out, busses were to become instrumental in my life. Rather an odd thought, but true. You see, as the rainy winter season progressed in Vancouver, I started to forego the chore of riding my bicycle to work in the cold and wet and splurged on taking the bus on a more frequent basis. Each morning I would wait patiently for the appropriate bus to arrive, get on, pay my fare and go sit in a seat by a window, keeping myself to myself. Then, one evening as I was heading home, the bus I climbed on board had a different driver...it was the driver that normally was on the morning bus!

"Hi there!" he said, smiling at me. He had a nice smile, was slim with brown hair, a beard and he had noticed me!

"Hello!" I automatically replied, rather red faced and somewhat taken aback as I headed to a seat. For the next few weeks, the routine was the same, seldom more than a

"Hi!" and "Hello!" passed between us although we did finally exchange names. Then, one evening as I handed over my fare, he asked, "So Rose, would like to go out to see a movie with me on Friday?"

"Yes! That would be lovely." I replied, blushing and nearly stammering at this sudden change of affairs. The remainder of the trip was spent sitting in the seat by the front door of the bus, chatting away as I gave him my address and we made plans to meet. I got off at my stop with a smile and a wave, walked the short distance home with what I am sure must have been a silly grin on my face. Finally, after all these years, I had been asked out on a "date"! A real date to go to the pictures! Now I had to figure out how to break the news to my father.

As it turned out, much to my great surprise, my father was very complacent about my impending evening out. Here I was, just about shaking in my shoes, telling him of the young gentleman, a local bus driver, who wished to take me to see a film in downtown Vancouver later that week. The evening finally arrived. A knock on the door signaled George was here.
"Good evening! You must be George," my father greeted him cordially, noting the fancy Volvo car parked at the curb. "Nice car you have there. All set to go, Rose? Remember, you need to be home by 10 p.m. or so." He waved as George and I pulled away from the curb.

The picture show was followed by a nice dinner in a small restaurant, a right treat for me I can tell you! Then, before I knew it, we were on our way back to my house. George seemed easy to talk to and it was a fun outing. After dropping me at the curb, I watched George drive away then entered the house to find my father sitting up waiting for me, a rather unpleasant look on his face. It was close to 11 p.m. and his words cut me to the quick.

"You're late. I thought I told you to be home by ten?" Then a smile crossed his face. Not a warm, welcoming smile, more of a sly grin as he said, "Don't worry Rose, I know why you were late, I have a very broad mind!" My eyes filled with tears, as I knew exactly what he was thinking! I was mortified.

"I don't know what you mean daddy! We saw a film and then had a bite to eat before he brought me home!" Here I was, only a little late and my father was implying... well I am sure you know what he was implying! I was devastated. My very first night out with someone and my father made me feel ashamed and dirty, even though all George and I had done was talk after we watched the film. I never even had a goodnight kiss!

That night was a turning point in my life. I had been seriously contemplating joining the Canadian Armed Forces with the idea of becoming an aircraft mechanic. Yes, that's right, an aircraft mechanic. Could it be that another path was opening up before me, a totally unexpected path? For shortly after our first outing, George asked me out again and soon we were seeing each other on a regular basis. My father had gone back to his cheerful self and never again alluded to what he surely still thought was going on. Then, after only a little over a month of seeing each other, George asked me to marry him, and I promptly accepted. It was not a flattering proposal, more like a business deal when I think back. Was I marrying for love? Maybe in my naive mind I thought I was, although deep down inside me I am sure there was a voice saying "Really? Are you sure or is this just an escape route? The coward's way out?" No, it must be for love, mustn't it? After all, he planned on flying me down to Texas to meet his family. He was going to pay for the entire wedding. He wants children, wants a wife who will cook and can and bake and... yes, this must be the right thing to do.

Sometimes as we sat and talked in his small apartment in downtown Vancouver, pictures came to my mind. I could imagine myself surrounded by children, cooking a nice Sunday dinner for my family, living on a couple of acres with chickens scratching outside the back door. A vegetable garden would lie a short walk down from the house where I would grow all the things my aunty Kay in England grows. Having a cellar, just like hers, in which all manner of home processed garden goodness was stored. Yes, I could see myself as a younger version of my aunty Kay. This must be the right thing to do, yes, it must be. When the coldness emanating from my father would wash over me on one of his bad days, I would close my eyes and see the vision of my perfect life before me. It sustained me, protected me and fortified me. Yes, it must be the right thing to do.

George seemed so full of life. He had travelled extensively and talked of us travelling too. Everything he said just convinced me more and more that this was the life for me, even when in a conversation one day he said in passing, "You know, If I had not met you, I think I would have gone to Utah to find a wife."
"Why on earth would you do that?" I replied.
"Well, I have a Mormon friend and his wife is the best housewife a man could have. She bakes, cans, knows how to do everything. They are so self-sufficient and independent. Real old fashioned they are." Odd thing to say I thought, but promptly put it out of my mind. I could bake and can and do all those things too. I was going to have a home and children and a long life with someone who loved me. So why was I still trying to convince a part of myself this was the right thing to do?

Chapter 2.

How quickly life can change. After coming home after yet another night out with George, showing my father the engagement ring on my finger, I thought my life had finally rewarded me with great happiness. My father raised a glass to toast us both. With tears in his eyes, he hugged me and his words filled me with joy,
"Oh Rose! All I have ever wanted in life was to see you happily married and taken care of." He seemed so jubilant, making plans to bake our wedding cake, thrilled that his little girl was going to be a bride! At least that was how it was at that moment; yes, how quickly life can change.

The happiness my father had was short lived. Before long, his attitude was that of a morose and surly man, angry and upset that his daughter would abandon him, leaving him all alone in the world. Nothing I could say would lift his spirits. No amount of tears and promising that he would forever be a part of my life seemed to matter. Was this not what he wanted for me? To be happily married? No, apparently not! He moped around the house. How often he would remind me of his sense of loss by saying,
"Everything I have done has been for you Rose. All the work over the years has been just for you. Look at all I have sacrificed! Look at what I have given up just for you."
"But daddy, I thought this is what you wanted? I thought you wanted me to marry George."
"Go on then, marry him. Forget about me. I'll manage somehow." He went on and on, reminding me over and over how his whole life had revolved around me. I felt guilty.

A trip to Texas to meet George's parents and sister – for he was an American by birth – was soon arranged. A trip that to me was both exciting and terrifying at the same time.

What would they think of me? Would they approve the marriage? As it was, the trip was uneventful. His parents were welcoming and his sister, Becky, made me feel right at home. It was a short first visit. Our picture was taken in the large living room of his parent's house, as it was customary in Texas for the engagement to be announced in the local paper. My fears of not being accepted by George's family were laid to rest as talk of wedding plans were fast and furious between Becky and my soon to be mother-in-law Betty. All I had to do was smile and nod a lot!

After returning home from our trip, George convinced me to move in with him. I am sure you can imagine the frightful rage with which my father heard the news! Surprisingly however, his anger did not last long, it seems as if he resigned himself to the fact that, in his words, he had lost his daughter forever. As quickly as his anger had come it passed, and he once again was acting as if he was glad I was getting married, even accepting my moving out in a very philosophical sort of way.

Our wedding date had been set for March 22nd of the following year, 1980. I was ready to get married right away but George set the date, stating it would be better for him tax-wise. Tax-wise? Now what on earth did that mean? Did I ask? No of course not! If that is what he wanted, then that is what we would do. I had received good training from my father. Do as you are told and avoid trouble. So when I learned Christmas was to be spent in Texas with his family, not at home in Vancouver with my father, it was all too easy to just do as I was told.

George just declared one day, "We're going to Texas to spend Christmas with my family."
"But what about daddy? I can't leave him alone for Christmas! What will he do here all by himself? I have never

14

spent a Christmas away from him before." I replied, tears stinging my eyes.

"Well, he can come down to Texas if he wants. My family needs to meet him anyway and I know they'll make him feel welcome...as long as he is civil!" Civil. George seemed to know my father's predilection for mood swings. Would my father be in one of his charmingly good moods with my future in-laws or would his sarcastic, acerbic side win out? When I asked my father about joining us, emphasizing how he had been invited, he said he would love to come. Then, as was his nature, at the very last minute he decided not to go, he would prefer to stay at home alone. This of course put me into a downward spiral of massive guilt! How could I go and have Christmas with comparative strangers when I knew my father would be all by himself? Many tears were shed but to Texas I went, feeling torn in half emotionally. Little did I know this would be a feeling I would become very familiar with.

Christmas and the New Year came and went. How quickly the wedding day approached! The church was booked, the reception hall and catering service reserved, guest invitations sent out, and my father still promised to bake a wedding cake to equal no other! But what a seesaw of emotions the past few months had been. Back in January my father declared he absolutely would not condone the wedding, would not attend, wanted no part of it at all, which of course devastated me! A few weeks later the tables again turned, and he was back to being enthusiastic about my upcoming nuptials – other than constantly insisting George and I move in with him afterwards to save money! Right up until a week or so before the Big Event he was so lighthearted. I on the other hand felt like a turkey being prepped for Christmas dinner!

George felt I was somewhat lacking in the womanly art of

skin care and make-up. It was apparently no longer appropriate to just wash my face with soap and water or pull my hair back into a simple ponytail. So I was sent off to some fancy cosmetician woman he knew who endeavoured to initiate me into the art of applying make-up – a hopeless cause – and who attempted to pluck my eyebrows – also a hopeless cause! I felt I was losing touch with Rose Forster. I was being molded into someone else and was unable to speak out, to object, it was too late.

My wedding gown – rented off the rack – was chosen for me. My hair, without my opinion being considered, was cut and styled. Do you know how scary it is to take off your glasses, being blind as a bat without them, and having someone do things to your hair that you cannot see until it is all done? I just wanted this all to be over. Then, another blow, a few days before the wedding, my father announced he had decided not to make my wedding cake; in fact, he would not be attending the wedding at all! What? No, no, no... this was not what I needed to hear! This could not be happening! How could he not want to be there, to walk me, his daughter, down the aisle? Feeling more than a wee bit frantic, I made my own wedding cake, a three-tiered affair, in our little cramped apartment. Cramped because my soon to be in-laws had arrived from Texas and were staying with us! George's father told me not to worry, he would walk me down the aisle if my father really chose to not show up, and it would all be okay. Really? Without my father there, how could it all be okay?

The day before the wedding, things did seem to fall into place. Well, other than George came down with a severe case of vertigo that almost had the wedding cancelled! He could barely stand, was nauseous and pasty faced, yet the wedding would continue, his mother would see to that! At the last minute my father arrived at the church, slipped a golden sovereign in my shoe for good luck and down the aisle I went. George somehow managed to keep on his feet, did not throw up, our vows were exchanged, and I became Mrs. Rose Ness.

After a brief honeymoon, we were back in downtown Vancouver, living in the tiny apartment at 1755 Haro Street just a few blocks from the renowned Stanley Park's Lost Lagoon. This had been George's bachelor flat for the past few years and where I had moved into before our marriage, assuming we would live here for quite a while longer. It was fun being a wife. Well, at least I thought so! George was meticulous about keeping an eye of his finances – notice I say his finances – and budgeted every last penny, but then I was well used to accounting for things. Given a weekly allowance for groceries, one of my great delights was making the choice to buy butter, yes, real butter, over margarine! My father and I spoke regularly on the telephone and we would often meet for a cup of tea and chat. He finally seemed to accept my marriage and appeared to be so very happy for me., Well, most of the time.

With George being a city bus driver, his bout of vertigo was such that he had a mandatory leave of absence from work for a few months until it was fully resolved. Taking advantage of being paid to stay off work meant there was plenty of time to travel. This was a grand time for me. George was, as I have mentioned, an American citizen although he chose to live in Canada. The next few months saw us making trips to many National Parks across America. We explored places such as Mesa Verde, Canyon Lands, Carlsbad Caverns, Yellowstone and the Grand Canyon plus, of course, a few trips down to Texas to visit his parents. Apparently, his occasional vertigo did not interfere with him driving us to and from these amazing places.

Finances became a little tight before George was cleared medically to return to work. During this time, my father had sold the old house on Manor Street and purchased another slightly more up-to-date dwelling not too far away, although still in the Vancouver suburb of Burnaby. After much discussion between George and me and major cajoling on my father's part, the decision was made for us to move into the finished basement of the new Burnaby house. I had great misgivings about this, as I did not want to return to living with my father. I was enjoying my sense of freedom far too much. On his part however, George thought it a good idea, as it would allow us to save money – it was always about money.

"Come on Rose! Moving in with your dad can't be all that bad? Look at all the money we can save while we live there. It will be no different than living on our own, will it? After all, he's your dad!"

Things were fine for a while, George congratulating himself on making the right move, me continuing to wait for the explosion I knew would come. Little by little the signs of discord were creeping up on us. For example, my father seemed to take great delight in making as much racket as possible in the early hours of the morning, knowing George was working night shifts so would be trying to sleep. This was just one of many ways he had of making our lives miserable. His other forte? Having the canny knack of making comments of a very suggestive nature, which invariably made me feel distinctly uncomfortable!

Finally, the disagreements – arguments to be exact – between George and my father became more frequent and the thought of saving money was far outweighed by the desire to once again have a place of our own. So, bags were packed, the meager furnishings George owned loaded into a rental moving van and back to Haro Street we went, thankfully finding a vacant apartment in the same building as before. I knew leaving my father's house had opened a rift between him and us, but George was sure it would just be a matter of time before my father would once again be knocking on our door. True enough, within a fortnight, acting as if nothing untoward had happened, my father telephoned for a chat. The rift had obtained a temporary patch.

It was good to be feeling like an independent person again, playing the role of wife and homemaker, for in some ways that is just what it felt like, play acting. However, I had a lot of obstacles to overcome and much to learn about being a wife. In my mind, George's friends seemed so very sophisticated, they, like George, were all around ten years or so older than me. When over to visit, they invariably would bring up fun times from the past, recalling times at parties, times when other women were mistress of George's apartment. It was hard to hear about his old girlfriends, even harder to see their pictures in his photo album! When I suggested one time if it would not be better to throw them away, I was shocked at his vehement refusal. Things came to a head with a right old row between us when I discovered a tape cassette lodged under the windshield wiper of his car. It was from one of George's former girlfriends, who I discovered was also from England, and whom he still had numerous photographs of. Taking it up to our apartment and placing it in our tape player, I was appalled to hear a homemade recording of music and personal thoughts of how much she was missing and still loved him. That did not make for a happy conversation between us when he got home from work! The honeymoon was over. Things were changing and niggling doubts as to if I had made the right choice in life started worming their way into my mind.

I had always been curious as to why someone born and raised in America would want to live in Canada, especially when his whole family, a family he was very close to, lived in the southern states. Yet George had made the choice to live in Vancouver, British Columbia, miles and miles away. One day he told me the story behind his move up north, an interesting tale. He had originally come to Vancouver to avoid being drafted into the military. The war in Vietnam was winding down and negative sentiment about being in the military ran high. George had no wish to be drafted, so his father, who was a career military man himself, managed to help him in this respect by some sort of paper shuffling with people he knew. George made his way from Texas to San Francisco then up to Seattle via an underground organization that helped people enter Canada who wished to avoid being drafted into the American Armed Forces. He was able to remain "on the run" for quite a while apparently, working as a cook in The Old Spaghetti Factory among other low paying jobs, until the day came when he had to make a major decision. He was up against the wall. If he did not return to the States and enter military service, his father might suffer consequences if it became known he aided and abetted his son's draft dodging attempt. So George returned to the States, joined the army and was sent to Guam where he was a clerk until his mandatory service was completed. Once discharged, he returned to Vancouver where he became a city bus driver, a job that paid well and gave him plenty of free time for travel.

Yes, there was much I came to learn about George – after we were married! Don't get me wrong, there were indeed great times during that first year together. Times when I truly thought I was living the good life! Any discord, any strife between us, I always laid the blame squarely at my own feet. I was young, inexperienced and naive. Surely it was my fault; I obviously was culpable when things went awry. Those frequent times when circumstances threatened to overwhelm me, I reminded myself of my wedding vows, those words I pledged, I was in this marriage for life, for better or for worse. No doubt it was up to me to work harder to make things better.

Chapter 3.

1980 seemed to pass so quickly. Before I knew it, I had
been married over a year, much travelling had been done
and I realized married life was not always a bed of roses!
George was back working full time and so it was decided I
also needed to get a paying job, but at doing what? Never
having attended college, I did not exactly have a specific career path in front of me. All I had been up to this point was
a shopkeeper with my father, a groom at a racetrack, a nanny and a butcher! None of which was exactly a well-paying
job nor one that George had in mind for me. Scouring the
employment ads in the newspaper, one came to the forefront and caught his, yes, his attention.
"Hey! This looks like a good one." He said, folding the paper and pushing it across the table to me, his finger point-
ing to a small advertisement.
"A manageress is needed for an exclusive European gift
shop in the Pacific Center mall?" I asked, raising my eye-
brow at the thought of me being a manageress.
"Why not? That sounds like a good job to me, after all,
you're from England. It's in the center of Vancouver, just
ten blocks from here. You could walk to work. You need to
go for an interview." Just like that the decision was made
for me.

George once again worked to make me look the part of a
manageress. Just before we were married, as I mentioned,
I was sent off to see a fancy cosmetician that he too frequented. This was supposedly to educate me in the matter
of skin care as up to this point in my life, my skin care had
consisted of washing my face vigorously with plain old
soap and water twice a day. I just could not get into all this
cleansing with a cleanser, washing with a different cleanser,
gently patting one's face dry then applying an astringent
followed by a day cream – or night cream depending on

time of day – and of course spritzing frequently with a "re-fresher" substance from a fancy brown bottle! No, this was not my cup of tea at all, yet it was something I had to do according to George, so of course I did it.

The person who owned the cosmetology shop was an older lady, originally from somewhere in Eastern Europe judging by her accent. The premises were very well appointed and gave the impression of opulence. Thick carpets on the floor, tasteful art on the walls and background music chosen to soothe and calm one's mind. Led into a small room with subdued lighting, warm cloths were gently placed on your face which soon had you feeling relaxed and pampered. The next half an hour was dedicated to the application of various creams and facial masks or being zapped with ultraviolet light, finishing up with lessons on the care of one's skin. Of course, one was expected to purchase all these fancy skin care products at what were to me, exorbitant prices!

Upon making it known one day that I thought it was silly to pay a small fortune for a supposedly "special" astringent sold in a fancy brown glass bottle that I knew was actually plain old witch hazel, well, you would have thought I had committed a deadly sin! I was never to criticize his cosmetician! Never, never, never! I was to do as I was told, wear what I was told and do my hair the way I was told. Gone were the days of shopping at the Salvation Army. Instead, George picked out what clothes I would wear, chose the hairstyle he felt suited me best. Did I complain? No, indeed I did not! Remember, I had been well taught by my father.

So, after a telephone call to set up an appointment for the manageress position, here I was, heading up a set of narrow stairs towards the head office of the Marc Singer gift shops. All set to have an interview with the owners, Marc and Heidi Singer. Smartly dressed in a new plaid skirt, white blouse and navy wool blazer, I firmly shook Mr. Singer's extended hand and the interview commenced. The result? I became manageress of their Pacific Center shop, the first of several establishments Marc and Heidi opened when they began their business in Vancouver many years ago.

This was a very special little shop, filled to the brim with all manner of wonderful things! As you entered the premises, you were transported from a modern underground shopping mall into another world in another time. The floor was made from very old wooden beams, oiled and buffed to a warm, dark hue. Shelves lined the walls and were filled with everything from beautiful pewter pieces to brightly polished brassware and crystal. Around the shop's center display, piles of burnished Turkish copper pots and pans were tastefully displayed and intricate wooden clocks from Switzerland hung on the wall to the left of the counter. In one of the front windows, artfully displayed, were beautiful hand carved decoy ducks, which caught the eyes of shoppers passing by.

There was something for everyone in this little shop. Exquisitely fine porcelain figurines from France, Spain and Italy drew one's eye from one shelf to another while delicate jade and ivory pieces lay nestled on a swath of velvet in a display case under glass. Collector plates are dotted here and there, tastefully displayed amid pewter tankards from Germany. Amongst all the candlesticks, vases and platters, was a certain item I had admired for over a year, a beautiful statue of a Thoroughbred horse. Designed by Helmut Diller of the Anri woodcarving studio in the Black Forrest region of Germany, carved from Linden wood, this statue was magnificent! I had passed by the shop numerous times when strolling through the mall, always pausing

to pear in the windows at the beautiful items on display.
When I first saw the figurine, I instinctively knew it would
be well beyond my means but was curious as to the price
for I had already named him, William Tell. However, I also
had perceived a very formidable looking blond-haired lady
attending the shop and did not have the nerve to enter and
enquire the price! Little did I know then that I would one
day be manageress of this very same shop and not only
that, but would be given that same beautiful horse for my
21st birthday present.

Close to five happy years passed in this little shop, tending it as if it were my own. Learning how and where each
item was made, the stories that made each item special to
the person who bought it. Coming to know and enjoy the
friendship of Doris and Ursula, the two other ladies who
worked in the shop. I became like a daughter to Doris, a
wonderful Swiss lady who introduced me to the wonders
of the opera and the love of silk – Doris wore nothing but
silk! Eventually I overcame my initial feelings of intimida-
tion and became good friends with Ursula, the seemingly
formidable blond haired German lady who had worked
for Marc and Heidi for years but had no interest in being
manageress. Most of all, this was where I would meet and
become lifelong pals with Marc and Heidi's niece, Cornelia. Yes, I loved this little shop and will always treasure my
time there.

My life basically revolved around working five days a week
– Tuesday through Saturday – in the little Marc Singer
shop and making a life for George and I in our tiny apartment. Sometimes my days off coincided with George's,
sometimes not. As a rule, Monday was my house cleaning,
laundry and shopping day. Most groceries were procured
by visiting the small shops found downtown, along the
streets adjacent to our apartment building. Occasionally

on a Sunday, a trip across town to other markets and shops
was made in order to restock our little kitchen. George
was very much into organic foods with whole grains and
vitamins being top of the list, but then it seems as if many
folk were during that time. Despite the extra cost, whenever possible I had to search for and purchase as much fresh
produce as possible with which to make our meals. I could
not use sugar for sweetening, honey only was the rule. No
white flour allowed in baking, just whole wheat. Nothing
with caffeine in it so there went my good old English tea!
Somehow herbal tea is not the same no matter how much
honey one puts in! It was a whole new way of cooking for
me and often a great challenge, but I persevered and somehow managed to keep decent meals on the table.

One of my greatest dislikes of this new regime, at least new
to me, was the daily consumption of a vast array of vitamin
tablets. Each morning and evening I would dole out our
daily ration of pills and capsules. 15 alfalfa tablets, vitamins E, D, various B's, papaya enzyme – I liked that one as
it tasted like a sweetie – vitamin C the size of a horse pill,
just to name a few. Topping it all off was washing them
all down with a full glass of green coloured, nasty tasting
chlorophyll tea. I am sure that is why I became allergic to
alfalfa later in life! There were so many pills to take each
day that I started making pictures with them on the kitchen
counter, flowers, horse heads and smiling sun faces. Who
needed breakfast after swallowing down that lot!

George's work schedule varied greatly. For a few months
he would be on a regular day shift, then it would change
and he would head out the door just as I arrived home
from work. Not having many friends to speak of evenings
often saw me spending a couple of hours a night riding
along on his bus route with him, just to pass the time.
Another occupation of mine was to grow a vegetable gar-

den on the tiny balcony we had. Pots were procured, filled with soil and seeds planted. There was not much room out there, but it sure was green and pretty, what with beans and peas climbing strings tied to the balcony above and lettuce and spinach overflowing their planters. During the summer, as a person walked along Haro Street, if they glanced upwards, they could see amongst the storied rows of bare balconies, a lone one, lushly festooned with healthy green plants!

Working in the little Marc Singer shop I was happy. On my days off however, if George were working on those days, I found myself becoming bored and restless. Living on the 12th floor of a high-rise apartment building in the center of a big city – albeit a very beautiful city – surrounded by people, noise and concrete, I found myself longing for the countryside. When first married, George had professed a desire to move to the countryside, owning a little house on a few acres where we could start a family, live off the land and in short, have an idyllic life. Somehow, something inside me was starting to realize this dream lifestyle might be far in the future and in fact, might never materialize at all. I missed having a dog and cat in my life but most of all I dearly missed horses. No matter where my father and I had lived in England, horses were an integral part of my life. I missed their smell, their companionship, the challenges and thrill of galloping over field and fence. I needed to have horses in my life, somehow I must find a way to have horses in my life again!

So one evening, sitting alone in our tiny apartment, I took up the telephone book and scoured through the yellow pages for any type of horse riding stables in the Vancouver area. There were many, but I had decided I would find a stable where I could take riding lessons. Not just any old lessons mind you, but dressage lessons and the instructor had to be an upper-level rider and instructor. Dressage had always been my weak point in my riding life. Galloping over a cross-country course, fearlessly jumping the imposing fences, that was my love. Dressage was just the "other" part of the Three-Day Event competition. A necessary but not very thrilling part, the area of my riding where I definitely felt lacking in skill. Yes, I would find a dressage instructor and improve that weak area in my riding. One name seemed to stand out to me, that of Patricia Deptford who owned Canterbury Farms. Without asking permission, as I knew George would think it frivolous, I called the number listed and made an appointment for a lesson with Patricia herself for the following Monday.

This was to be a turning point, not only in my equine education, but also in me myself. Maybe it was a streak of rebelliousness finally coming to the surface. By hook or by crook I was going to find a way to be with horses, even in the middle of a city! As I sat there after making the call and committing to a lesson, that old nemesis Fear started to worm its way into my mind. Questions and doubts assailed me,
"What had I done? What will George say?" I trembled inside at the thought of telling him.
"What can he say? You earn a good wage each month and see hardly a penny of it!" the voice of reason tried to calm me. "He goes off skiing whenever he wants to doesn't he? Surely you can have a little fun too?"
"But what if he tells me I can't. What if he gets cross with me?" the back-and-forth conversation seemed to go on for ages in my mind. I would just tell him I am going to start riding lessons and stick with it no matter what. Surely he will not mind.

Actually, it was easier than I imagined, telling George I had decided to take a riding lesson or two on my days off.

He was surprisingly fine with the idea; even showing me which bus routes would be the best to get me there. What on earth had I been so afraid of! The anticipation and yes, apprehension of meeting new people was tempered by the fact that once more I could be around horses, here, in the middle of a city.

Chapter 4.

Horses have always been a huge part of my life and living in the middle of a big city, I never would have thought a way could be found for that to continue. Goodness knows how long I was going to be ensconced in a small apartment on the 12th floor of a high-rise apartment building! However, where there is a will there is a way as they say. Despite feeling sure George would put a damper on my plan of spending money on riding lessons, being pleasantly surprised when he agreed to the idea, I plunged ahead and looked forward to my first introductory lesson with Patricia Deptford. As owner of the Canterbury Farm riding stables, she taught out of the Southlands Riding Club located on the southern fringe of Vancouver itself. Taking the bus, since George always drove the car to and from work, I must have looked an unusual sight in my anorak, jodhpurs and riding boots with my helmet tucked under my arm.

Finding the stable was easy enough after a short walk from the bus stop. I reveled in the smells of barnyards, hay and horse manure! Upon reaching the yard, a young lady by the name of Yolanda Blommers, set me up with a horse and sent me on my way down the lane for my lesson with Patricia. It was an intimidating affair I can tell you, for here I found my future instructor, sitting in the corner of the arena, bundled up against the cold, balancing on a shooting stick.
"So, tell me about your riding capability." She asked.
"Well, I have ridden most of my life, mainly other people's horses you understand. I went through Pony Club in England, competed in three-day events, rode point to pointers…" I felt I was not doing a very good job presenting my experience to her, I felt intimidated, as if it would be boasting to name the competitions I had ridden in. She proceeded to ask numerous more questions then put me

through my paces, requesting half-pass, shoulder in, flying changes, extended trot and other common dressage maneuvers. I no longer felt intimidated but gave myself up to the feeling of being astride a fine horse, letting the sensation of controlled power thrill me to the core!

Nearing the end of my hour lesson, I rode up to Patricia to hear the verdict of if she would take me on as a student. Her evaluation of my riding technique hit me like a ton of bricks, what a blow to my ego! As she sat there on her shooting stick, no warm smile crossed her face. Instead, her words sure wiped the smile off my face as she said, "Well, I can see you can sit a horse, but you are not having a cup of tea with the Queen!" I stared at her in disbelief as she went on.

"There is certainly no need to crook your little finger up when holding the reins as if you are holding a cup. Your seat might be fine for jumping fences but has much to be desired in the dressage arena!" What? Who on earth was this lady to tell me such things? I had competed in some of England's major competitions and held my own. I had ridden most of my life! Okay, so I know in the area of dressage I had weaknesses, but really, was I that bad? She commenced talking as I sat there red faced.

"I will, however, take you on as a student. It will work into my schedule to see you every Monday. Though, to ride with me you will need to become a member of the Southland's Riding Club. See you next Monday." And with that, she got up, folded her shooting stick, tucked it under her arm and walked out of the arena.

After riding back to the stable yard, untacking and taking care of my horse, I stomped off to catch the bus home. I was fuming! Then with reflection, came the rueful acknowledgment that this lady was right. I had ridden by the seat of my pants for years, now I needed to have refinement and, yes, Pat would be the person to help me. But what was I going to say to George? Lessons alone were what to me at the time was a whopping sum of $25 per hour. Then there was the fee to join the riding club, which was over $300 for an annual membership! George would never agree to that. But this was something I really wanted and really needed to do. It would be my weekly escape from the confines of the city and, after all, I was making a nice salary at Marc Singer's so surely I should be able to do this.

Thinking of how I would present things to George, my arguments paid off and my weekly trips to ride made the following few years more bearable. My dressage improved rapidly, I even was able to fit in some jumping, riding some of Pat's young horses for her. An added bonus was being able to bring home a token from the farm each Monday in the form of a black plastic rubbish bag substantially filled with ripe yet well-composted horse manure for my little balcony garden! Here I thought I had received funny looks in my jodhpurs and boots! You can image the looks I got when I was accompanied by the distinct odor of horse manure too... not that it bothered me in the slightest!

Yes, my weekly jaunts to ride were truly the highlight of my time in Vancouver, for increasingly I was becoming more and more discontent with my life. I enjoyed my work in the little shop, but my home life was sometimes a bit challenging. Maybe I was growing up, finally seeing life not as a young girl but as a married woman and as such, was discovering a little more about myself.

During my early years as Rose Ness, my father was in and out of my life, an odd thing to say, but true. For a while we would see each other on a regular basis, talking on the telephone, having him popping now and then into the shop to say hello. We would go from one day being a loving father and daughter then all of a sudden he would become cross about something or other and I would not hear from him for ages. These silent times always made me feel terribly guilty. Made me feel he was upset because I was with my husband and not with him, making me feel as if I had abandoned him after all he had sacrificed for me. This would put me in a state of turmoil. Did he want me to choose between him and my husband? No, surely he would never put me in that position would he? On the other hand, George would run out of patience with me trying to rationalize my feelings of guilt about my father.

"You are a grown woman and married now!" he would remind me. "Why don't you act like it and stand up to him?"

"But you know how he is George. I can't talk to him like you can to your mum and dad. I can't tell him how I feel. He will just get even more angry with me. Don't you understand?" As usual when I got upset, the tears came quickly to my eyes. I felt as if I was torn between two worlds, dutiful daughter on one hand and wife on the other. Thankfully, it was around this time that Marc and Heidi's niece, Cornelia, came to work in the little shop. Cornelia and her family were to become a second family to me and in many ways, kept me grounded.

Cornelia was the middle child of a lovely German couple, Hans and Edith Koch. Cornelia's older brother Frank and Riki, her younger sister, became my surrogate family. After they immigrated to Canada from Turkey, where they had lived for many years, they settled themselves in West Vancouver. I loved going over to Cornelia's house. A very close-knit family, it was here I was exposed to new foods, a new culture and most of all, a sense of what a family should be. There was an easiness between them that is hard to explain. Frank, Cornelia and Riki would not hesitate to voice their opinions to their mum and dad; a mild disagreement, which started in English, could erupt into a bout of German in an instant and be over as quickly as it began. They were a truly sophisticated and well-educated family. Their home was filled with stunning artwork, richly coloured Turkish rugs, beautiful copper pieces gleamed everywhere; it was like entering another world, a very European world.

Cornelia was one of those rare people who could throw on a pair of jeans, an old sweatshirt and look like she just stepped out of a fashion magazine. She had an impeccable taste for fine clothes, and through her my wardrobe expanded to include classical wool skirts, crisp linen blouses, warm cashmere sweaters and fine leather shoes. How could I afford such clothes you may wonder? Well, she was also a canny shopper, hitting the very best shops when their wares were on sale at seemingly ridiculously low prices. I came to appreciate the value and durability of quality over quantity. George saw the usefulness of such a friend and became quite generous in my clothing allowance. Soon wool and cotton and soft spun cashmere jumpers replaced polyester and synthetic garments in the clothes cupboard. Where once I lived in running shoes and wellies, my footwear now comprised of strappy high heel sandals and smart leather pumps with handbags to match.

What grand times and many laughs Cornelia and I had when working together in our little shop down in the mall. Like the time I fainted, for some unknown reason, just as Aziz the older stockman gentleman was coming into the shop to deliver goods to replenish the shelves. One minute I was standing behind the counter talking to Cornelia and saying hello to Aziz, the next minute I was flat on my back on the floor! Or the time I nearly squashed Cornelia as she was sitting in the tiny narrow room, tucked away from sight at the back of the shop where odds and ends were stored and where we could sit and eat our lunch. She was perched on the stool that just fit in the narrow room, watching me as I brought the little wooden stepladder back behind the counter. I needed to reach something from high on the back shelf and carefully maneuvered the ladder in the narrow space between the counter and the back wall. As Cornelia munched away on her lunch, I set the ladder in place and proceeded to climb up the few steps. Much to both of our surprise – for I had forgotten to open the ladder completely – it slowly and steadily started to fall, with me clinging to it, straight towards Cornelia who, in the tiny little storage space, had nowhere to escape! Thankfully I crashed to the ground unharmed and missed Cornelia by inches!

We were great pals ... and still are to this very day. She was a person I could confide my deepest worries and feelings to. She was compassionate and caring, my lifeline when the world seemed to be crashing down on me. The person I could vent all my frustrations and fears to. Someone much wiser than her years, for despite me being older and married as well, it was Cornelia who I often felt had the more mature head on her shoulders. She was my dear friend and my harbour in the storm. It turned out I would need that comforting harbour sooner than I thought.

Chapter 5.

Much happened in my life between 1980 and 1985. Those five years in some ways seemed to pass by quickly and in others went at a snail's pace. My life had assumed a pretty steady routine, working five days a week in the little shop, riding lessons with Pat on most Mondays, juggling my relationship with my father and my husband. Interspersed with this were outings with Cornelia such as our taking up evening pottery classes at a local community college and the "Yoga for Riders" class – at which Cornelia gamely joined me – put on by a wispy little woman called Zarda and held at the Southland's Riding Club on a Thursday evening. Yet under the surface of this seemly mundane existence, currents were stirring which would have a huge impact on my life for many years to come.

George was spending more time on night shift bus routes than day routes it seemed. Yet we still had occasional days off together which we filled with shopping excursions and the occasional visit with my father – when my father and I were on speaking terms, that is! Holidays were invariably spent in Texas at his parents' home in Georgetown. It was a totally different world down in Texas. My first trip down there for Christmas was an eye-opener! It was incredibly strange to be wearing shorts and a t-shirt because of how warm it was outside in what should be the middle of winter. Then there was Christmas dinner. My first such dinner at my in-law's house was, shall we say, different! The turkey was familiar and standard fare, but all the other dishes were not!
"Where are the Brussels sprouts?" I whispered to George as we filled our plates at the formal dining room table.
"What do you mean?"
"Well, the real potatoes, parsnips and carrots, forcemeat stuffing and Christmas pudding and custard for dessert?"

My unfortunate comment to George was met with strong
disfavor! The table was laid out with an array of jelly type
salad dishes which looked more like dessert to me.
"These sweet potatoes things have marshmallows on
top!" His sharp glance was enough to make me be quiet.
So, I politely tried the green bean casserole topped with
crunchy things and managed to swallow down some very
interesting stuffing the likes of which I had never tasted.
Instead of Christmas pudding and custard for dessert there
was pecan pie and ice cream! Nothing like the traditional
English Christmas dinner I was used to at all!

Texas, as I say, was quite a different place to experience.
I never felt totally at home in my in-law's house although
they showed me nothing but kindness. Everything had its
place and was always neat and tidy. My mother-in-law, a
tiny little woman with a formidable personality, was what
I came to consider the perfect housewife. Everything was
immaculate. No dust, no mess, no pillow out of place on
the settee. The garden was perfectly manicured; the garage
so clean one could eat off the floor! Yes, everything was
perfect. I must have been a wee bit of a surprise to them, a
young girl who liked insects, delighted in collecting lightening bugs in a jar, had no fear of the tarantulas or local
snakes and was determined to catch one of the armadil-
los that frequented the garden. In fact, so fascinated was
I by the insects that abound down there, that I was given
a book titled "The Most Dangerous Insects and Animals
of the Southwest." This being after I was about to pick up
a huge centipede from the living room floor, scaring my
mother-in-law half to death! Texas is definitely not a place I
wanted to live, too hot and too dry with too much air-con-
ditioning everywhere. George was content to pop down to
visit, but he too had other places in mind to live.

Less than a year after we were married, George decided

that one day in the not-too-distant future, we would move
to America. He was, in a lot of ways, a very different fellow.
An anti-establishment, anti-government, want-to-be surviv-
alist sort of chap you might say. There was no cable television hooked up in our apartment – although cable was
supplied as part of our apartment rent – because he had
read the government could "spy" on you through the cable
lines, even if your television was not turned on! So although we did have a small television with an aerial, it was
in an entertainment center and the doors had to remain
closed when the telly was not on. How often I was reminded of this fact.

"Rose, haven't I told you before to keep those doors
closed? The government wants to see what everyone is
doing! One of these days there will be nuclear war in the
world and we have to prepare for that. I know. I saw things
when I was in Guam!" he would remind me, over and over
again.

"Yes George, sorry George. I'll remember that, George." I
would reply, sighing as I shut away the television screen by
closing the cupboard doors.

While George was still off work on sick leave right after we
were married, I cannot count the number of hours spent
in the local library researching all manner of odd things.
George was trying to decide where in the western states we
should plan on eventually moving to, for even then he was
considering leaving Vancouver. Apparently in Guam, where
he had been stationed during his stint in the military, he
had discovered, supposedly, a number of facilities in the
west of the United States that were considered prime tar-
gets for a nuclear attack. Naturally, the majority were large
cities such as Seattle, Portland, San Francisco et cetera. Not
wanting to be anywhere in the vicinity of those places – for
he was certain the day would come in the not-too-distant

future when a nuclear strike against North America would happen – we thereby had to find a "safe" place to reside. But where would we go?

Over the next year, escape routes from Vancouver were calculated and planned out. An emergency pack for each of us was under the bed stocked with clothing, some money, a little dried food, important papers, toiletries and such. I was given all manner of books to read – ordered to read them actually, whether I wanted to or not – on how the government was corrupting our food supply, manipulating the economy, compromising our health. Books on how the pharmaceutical industry in conjunction with the food industry is committed to keeping people in a state of poor health. The list was long! Not exactly enjoyable reading, but, as usual, I did as I was told.

Poring over weather maps that gave historical data on wind patterns, pinpointing nuclear power plants, looking at rainfall data, days of sunlight – the list seemed endless. However, one additional, and very major factor we had to keep in mind, was that whatever place it turned out to be where we might eventually move to, it must have a ski area. Ski area? Oh, right! George was an avid downhill skier so of course he must have a ski area close by. How silly of me! Notes were compiled, checked and re-checked; circles drawn on road maps until finally the list was narrowed down to two possible locations. Bend, Oregon and Kalispell, Montana.

Kalispell is a beautiful city in the northern area of Montana and considered the gateway to the stunning Glacier National Park. It looked so charming in the travel magazines and books. Numerous ski resorts were close by and even if the climate did not seem overly conducive to growing a garden, a person could get around that by having a greenhouse. Not too populated, a place artists and the like seemed to congregate, yes, George thought this might be the place. So a trip was made, real estate agents contacted, the area thoroughly looked over, the ski area visited even though it was summer. The drawback was land and house prices were higher than what we could afford.

The next place to visit on the list was Bend, Oregon. Bend in the early 1980s was still a relatively small town; seemingly very rural, yet had all the amenities of a much larger city. Lots of farms lay on the outskirts and it was very sunny, supposedly the sunniest place in the state of Oregon! Nestled on the east side – the dry side – of the foothills of the Cascade Mountains, Bend is a very picturesque place. The mountains, lakes, resorts and golf courses make this a great tourist destination. Not only that, but Mount Bachelor ski resort was, and still is, one of the best in the west. Since I did not ski that did not make a big impression on me! The economy at that time was still growing and more importantly, house and land prices seemed affordable. "This is it!" George declared. "This is the place we will be moving to. We can find a house on a little bit of land and one of these days we will live here." Little did I know that "one of these days" was to happen a mere five years later in 1985… but I am getting ahead of myself here.

After our trip to Bend, George started communicating with a number of real estate agents and ended up finding a little fixer-upper house on a couple of acres in Tumelo, a small community just on the outskirts of Bend. Another trip was made to look the property over, and George made the decision to buy. The little house was in much need of repair. The land was fenced although the pastures were overgrown with weeds. There were water irrigation rights, which we had been told was a great asset, and so the place had promise. The surrounding properties were irrigated with lines of huge sprinklers and in the green fields horses and cattle grazed. Yes, there were possibilities here. I could see myself on this place. My dream of a large, loving family, dogs, cats, a garden and orchard flared in my mind. Surely we could be happy here. A fine place to raise our children, for that is what I longed for the most.

Once the sale was finalized – the actual purchase price never being revealed to me –another trip from Vancouver to Bend was made. The few days we spent there were frantically filled with cleaning up the place. Washing then painting the interior walls bright white and the exterior of the house a sunny yellow. A rental agency was retained and they quickly found a family to rent the property, the rent supposedly covering the mortgage payment. How naïve I still was not daring to ask more about the financial side of things! Of course, my name was not on the house deed, no indeed not! For as George told me, only an American could own property in the United States. Silly me, I believed him! "The house was purchased on a Land Sales Contract, Rose. You can't have your name on something like that since you are not American." He would tell me.
"So even if we move down here I can't own anything?"
"I have already told you, no!"
"Can we afford a house in Bend as well as paying our rent here in Vancouver?" I persisted.
"Don't worry. It's all figured out. The payment we get from the renters pays what is owed to the person who sold us the house. They in turn make payments on the underlying mortgage they have on the land. Nothing could be easier that that! Stop worrying," he said. So why was I still feeling uneasy about this? Somewhere inside me I just knew this was a mistake!

All seemed to be going well. I was working, George was working again and each month a payment was sent off down to the states to pay for the little house and land. Unfortunately, it was not going to be too long before things took a turn for the worst. Interest rates in the early 1980s took a major upward swing. Fine if you had money in the bank, not so good if you had an adjustable-rate mortgage! One day, sometime in early 1983, a letter arrived in the post from a solicitor's office in America, informing us that the little house in Tumelo was about to be repossessed by the bank that held the underlying mortgage. What? How could that be? Payments had been sent off each month without fail to the person the house had been bought from! Well, it was brought to our attention that the person who had been receiving those payments George sent down had not been bothering to pay the underlying mortgage payments as was supposed to happen. Ah! The catch of a Land Sales Contract! One was trusting on the other party be honest and carrying through on their part of the bargain! So all of a sudden, if we wanted to keep the little house in Tumelo, we had to come up with the full cost of the underlying mortgage held by the mortgage holder or lose not only the property but also all the money we had paid out each month! The sum? A total approaching close to $53,000 American dollars! Where on earth were we going to get that sort of money?

In all honesty, I had no idea how much money we actually had. Only George had his name on the bank accounts, he handled the chequebook and I had no idea what was in savings. I never knew where the down payment came from – or how much it was – that had been paid out for the property in Tumelo. Each payday George took my cheque, and I was given a certain amount of cash money to cover household expenses and that was that. The one thing I did know was that we did not have such a sum as was needed just lying around the place. It was a grim situation. We had nothing to use a collateral and besides that, interest rates had jumped to over 18 percent almost overnight! What on earth could we do?

George had the idea of turning to my father.
"Why don't we ask your dad if he can help us out? We could explain the situation and see if he would be willing to loan us some money." I could not believe George was actually considering such a thing!
"George! Why would you even want to ask him? No, no, no … that is not a good idea!" I was vehemently opposed to this suggestion. Losing the property and all money paid into it was more appealing than being beholden to my father!
"George, you don't know him like I do! We would be under his thumb; under his power you might say and that thought terrifies me! I know what he is like." I could actually feel myself shaking at the thought. We argued back and forth.
"But as long as we made our payments on time to him, what hold could he have over us?" George reasoned. No matter what I said, I could not convince him this was a bad idea. No not bad, a terrible idea.
"Please, please, please do not do this!" I begged, for I could see no good coming from this arrangement.
"Oh, come on Rose! He's offered to help us in the past. We'll write something up, a promissory note or something, just as if we borrowed the money from a bank. It will be the same! We'll even pay him interest. Don't worry about it!" he replied, ignoring my protests. No matter what I said it made no difference and I finally gave in, and my father was asked if he could help us out.

I do not think I will ever forget the look on my father's face when we poured out our tale of woe to him, asking for his help. It was almost one of satisfaction. We only had a very short window of time to come up with the money before the foreclosure proceedings started and he was thrilled to help us!

"Sure, I can help you. In fact, I'll give you the money. After all, what good is it doing me sitting in the bank?" he said, smiling at us as he puffed away on his cigarette. I had no idea my father had such a sum he could lay his hands on just like that. I was thinking he would somehow be able to help us out with just a portion of the funds and then we could try to get a loan or something for the rest. The one thing I most certainly did not want, however, was to be given the money. My father never just gives; he always wants something in return!

"If we were to do this, daddy, borrow money from you," I said, "there would be a proper promissory note drawn up, we would make monthly payments"

"And pay you interest too." George added.

"We can just shake hands, but if you want to do things properly and draw up a note, that is fine with me." My father replied. What huge misgivings I had when all three of us signed that note! The interest was set at 10%, so much better than 18%, the funds transferred to George's account and the payment made to the bank in America for the little house in Tumelo. The deed was recorded in George's name only since, remember, he had told me I could not own property in the United States because I was not a citizen!

The stress of this whole episode was huge to me. Now my father had a very significant hold over us, a hold I do not think George fully comprehended at the time. Stress brought out tension, which led to arguments and discord in our marriage. Money was tight yet we still had to make trips down south on a regular basis to visit his family. Thank goodness I had my pal Cornelia and old school chum Kim on whose shoulders I could reliably cry on when things became rough. Kim I could only write my

woes to as she lived in northern Canada, Cornelia was
my close port in a storm and escaping occasionally to her
house was balm to my soul! Yet something else quite miraculous happened that was to profoundly make its mark
on me.

My father was an avid dancer and always had been. During
our first trip west to Vancouver, British Columbia, back in
late 1973, we lived for a good while on skid row. There,
as a diversion, my father found a love of square dancing.
While I would stay safely ensconced in our little room at
the Glenaired Hotel on Granville Street, butcher knife
under my pillow for protection, he would be off dancing
somewhere. Soon, square dancing and then round dancing
became a passion of his. Always a spectacular and talent-
ed ballroom dancer, this switch of form was easy for him
and also brought him lots of lady partners! One day, late in
1982, I received a telephone call from my father that was to
shake my world to the core. He had, apparently, been looking for a dance hall in the telephone book when he came
across the name "Fleig, T." Now Fleig is not at all a common surname and there was only one Fleig in the book so
my father dialed the number, curious as to if this could be
a Tommy Fleig he had known many years ago in Montreal.
When the 'phone was answered, my father asked,
"Is this Tommy Fleig? The Tommy Fleig who once lived in
Montreal?"
"Yes" the person replied, "Who is this?" to which my father
then went on to say, "This is Tommy Forster. Do you remember me? I was married to your mother."
Oh yes, yes indeed Tommy Fleig remembered him, for
Tommy Fleig was none other than my brother.

Thankfully, my father had called the one brother of mine
who would give him the time of day and be civil to him.
Had he called either of my older brothers, David or Char-

lie, the reception would not have been so cordial! After chatting with Tommy for a brief while, my father gave me a ring and passed along the news ... very shocking news. "Rose!" he said when I picked up the receiver, "I have some good news for you. I was looking for a dancehall called Fleetwood and came across the name of Fleig in the telephone book. I recognized the name and since it's an unusual one, I gave them a ring. Can you believe it? It was one of your brothers." What? One of my brothers? What on earth was he talking about?

"What do you mean daddy, 'one of my brothers'?" I felt wobbly, a bit sick inside.

"You have three brothers and one of them lives right here in Vancouver." Did I hear him right? I have three brothers? "Oh, and by the way, I found out your mother is dead. Well, I am off, I'm running late so will talk to you later." With those words he rang off and I was left clutching the receiver to my ear.

I felt as if the air had been sucked out of my lungs, tears prickled at my eyes, I felt sick to my stomach. I had three brothers? Bursting into tears, I passed the news on to George. My heart was aching, not just from the news of having brothers out there, but because my mother was dead. All of a sudden I felt a great, empty hole in my heart, a wound that was deep and raw and so very, very painful. Why should I be feeling this way? A part of my mind tried to tell me "You didn't know her, she was the ogre woman, she didn't want you remember?" Yet deep inside me I suddenly knew this was not true, could not be true, my heart could not be aching so badly if this was true! No, no, no this couldn't be true! Yet inside I knew it was, I had lost my mother and now I would never get the chance to get to know her, to talk to her, to learn about her. For some reason, one I could not quite fathom, a short while before I was married, I had been hankering to find and contact my mother. Something inside me wanted to find her, to get to know her.

That is why, just before I was married, I had the urge, no, let me rephrase that, a strong, burning desire to have my mother at my wedding. Not knowing how to contact her myself, I asked my father if he might know how to contact her.

"Daddy? Do you think my mother would want to come to my wedding? Do you know how I could get hold of her?"

"Why would you want to do that?" my father said, looking a bit disconcerted.

"I don't know, I just really want to tell her about the wedding." His next words surprised me.

"I know where she lives. If you are sure about this, why don't you make out an invitation and I'll pop it in the post for you." Not quite knowing what to say, I wrote a short note explaining to my mother how much I would like to have her come to my wedding, that I felt I wanted to get to know her after all these years. Waiting impatiently for a response, which never came, only reinforced in my mind that she truly did not want anything to do with her little girl.

"She didn't even have the decency to write to me to tell me she would not come to my wedding!" I complained to George. Why then, should I be feeling so sick inside, so devastated at the news my mother had passed away? It made no sense. No sense that is until I learned later, from my brothers, that my mother had passed away a few years earlier. That was not the worst of it, my father knew when my mother had died, yet he never told me, never let me know until after I was married. I had lost my chance to get to know the woman who gave me life, the woman I never got the opportunity to know, the woman who I am part of.

Many, many years later, I was to discover my father routinely sent pictures of me, school pictures mostly, to my mother.

Chapter 6.

Get rich quick! Sounds great but, like so many things in life, if it sounds too good to be true it probably is! Life was steadily plodding along in Vancouver. A routine had established itself in my life, comprising of work, Monday riding lessons with Pat, grocery shopping and house cleaning, spending time with Cornelia and her family when George was at work and occasionally meeting my father for a cup of tea and chat. Routine is good I would tell myself; it tends to take one's mind off the not so good things in one's life. Routine would become my friend, as here in 1983, a trying year, I was finding a number of not so good things entering my life.

Living under the cloud of owing money – a lot of money – to one's father, feeling as if one is living slightly beyond one's means is a tad stressful to say the least! This must have also been on George's mind as we now entered the "Get rich quick!" phase of our life together. I am not sure if it was a common occurrence in those days, for I was not exactly on top of current affairs of the world, but it seemed as if suddenly there was an upsurge in interest in folks purchasing real estate. George was forever bringing home brochures on seminars that would teach you how to profit from buying real estate. Topics such as "Buy Houses for $1 Down!" or "Make Money in Real Estate!" To me, the only one making easy money was the person standing on the stage who collected the couple of hundred dollars from each person who was suckered in to attending his lecture on how he got rich quick! George was determined to go to these seminars, spending not only the money to attend but buying the "self-help" tapes and books that was guaranteed to turn our lives around! Nothing I could say seemed to make a difference in his determination to make this work. Somehow, the thought of buying an old fixer-upper house, renovating it and then selling it for a huge profit or better yet, renting it out for easy income was intoxicating to him! To me, all I could see was that it was going to take money to make money and, unfortunately, we did not have any extra money stored away. Instead, we were deep in debt and there was no way I was going to go back to my father to borrow more! Finally, I just flat out refused to go with him to any of these shyster seminars! George was not at all happy about that!

We were still making a couple of trips a year down south to visit my in-laws and occasionally we would head to Bradenton Beach, Florida, to visit George's grandparents. They were good folks, living in a tiny little bungalow, not too far from the beach. George's grandfather was suffering from dementia and the early stages of Alzheimer's. A quiet, gentle old man, I would sit with him for what seemed like hours, just listening to him talk and paying him attention since I sometimes felt the rest of the family did not. George's grandmother was a busy little lady, her house filled to the brim with all manner of plants and glass knick-knacks, odds and ends she had found on the nearby beach. She was like a little bright-eyed bird who loved shiny things and always thought she had room for one more treasure in their overstuffed nest!

It was on the way home from one of these excursions to Florida that George had the idea we should make a trip to the Bahamas.
"I've been reading this book on off-shore bank accounts." He said as we drove down a long stretch of highway.
"What, like a Swiss bank account?" I asked.
"Yes, but they have them in the Bahamas too. I was thinking we should make a trip to Nassau one of these days soon." I immediately thought of tropical beaches and clear blue waters to swim in, he was thinking about opening an

offshore Swiss bank account!

"Really? What on earth are we going to deposit in a Swiss bank account? We don't exactly have an abundance of spare cash lying around!" I could see by the tightening of his lips that I had made a blunder in my skeptical answer. The conversation abruptly ended, and I resumed my vacant staring out the car window. Oh well, it would be a trip to somewhere I had never been before I thought. I duly obtained a Canadian passport – I was officially a Canadian citizen due to my father becoming one the last time we immigrated to Canada – and a trip to Nassau in the Bahamas was planned. It was only going to be a short trip, and do I mean short! Drive to Florida, Miami to be exact, fly to the Bahamas one day, stay the night and following day then fly back to the States before driving back to Vancouver. A day would be spent going around to various banks enquiring about offshore accounts. Sounded simple enough, so why could I see so many flaws in this plan?

The drive to Florida was fast but uneventful. The flight from Miami to Nassau short. The sun hot and the colours bright! After finding a cheap boarding house and renting a tiny little room, we proceeded to walk in the blazing heat to the main business area of the city. Somehow, the banks looked intimidating. Around us were the bright colours and smiling faces of the local inhabitants, a sharp contrast to the austere looking buildings and the uniform clad bank security guards! Entering the cool, air-conditioned building George asked to see the new accounts manager. A young concierge politely escorted us to a seat where we sat waiting to be seen, me at least feeling very out of place. Soon, an impeccably dressed gentleman came forward and introduced himself, leading us back to his private office where he proceeded to enquire how he could help.

Now I had my misgivings about this idea before we even

set foot on Bahamian soil. Although I did not know anything about banking, I did know that when you heard about Swiss bank accounts, it usually was in conjunction with very rich people or gangsters! We did not fit into either category! Somehow, I did not feel it was going to be as simple as opening an account at the local credit union, and I was right. George proceeded to ask the details of opening an account, the safety of such an account, how easy was it to transfer money into and out of said account et cetera. Then it was the turn of the bank associate to explain the banks requirements. I had an idea he saw immediately that we had no idea of what having a numbered Swiss account actually meant! There was an actual cost, not inconsiderable by any means, just to open an account. Couple that with annual fees for the privilege of having an account with them and of course a minimum deposit was required. The meager amount George had planned to deposit, I recall it being less than $500, would barely have covered the fee to even open an account! We were way out of our league and the bank associate knew it. He was polite, gave George a brochure and, needless to say, we rose, thanked the gentleman for his time and left without opening an account. Realizing the same story would be repeated at any other financial institution we visited, George gave up the idea and we headed to the boarding house with the intent of changing clothes and heading to the beach for the remainder of the day.

Ah! What a beach! Lovely white sand, sparkling clear turquoise water, loads of people tanned to perfection and here was us, white as can be under the scorching sun. I myself am not and never have been, someone who likes to sunbathe on the seashore. I like to swim. To me, going to the seaside means swimming in the sea. George on the other hand was content to lay on the sand although admonishing me to watch out for dangerous fish and the nasty cone snails which he said inhabited the shallow waters. The water was delightful and felt good on my skin after the blistering heat of the sun.

While I was enjoying floating along in the gentle surf, I noticed a very lovely looking lady had arrived and proceeded to sit down beside George on the beach. They were laughing and chatting away like old friends as I left the water and walked up to say hello. George did not at first introduce me. He ignored my presence as a matter of fact, it was only when the lady looked up at me inquiringly that he begrudgingly made introductions.
"Oh, this is Rose." He said, as if we were mere friends and not married. The lady instantly dismissed me, continuing with her conversation as if I was non-existent. She was quite a good-looking woman, well-tanned and well-endowed in all the right places if you know what I mean, her curves shown to advantage by a rather skimpy bikini. In comparison I felt rather like an old dowager in my one-piece Speedo swimming costume! Stubbornly plonking myself on the sand beside them, they continued chatting for a bit although totally ignoring me. Before long, the woman rose gracefully to her feet.
"So, I will see you later on?" she said before walking away, looking only at George.
"Sure, I'll be there! Catch you later!" he replied with a grin.

As we gathered up our things and started walking back to the rooming house, I could not hold my tongue any longer.
"What on earth did she mean, 'later on'?" I could feel my temper rising!
"We have been invited to a party on the beach this evening. That's all. I was just making conversation with her while you were in the water. No big deal!" he replied, rather impatiently.

"We or just you?" I asked.

"Well, she didn't actually mention you but I'm sure you could come along if you wanted to. I thought you didn't like parties." My heart plummeted. No, I did not want to go to some party on the beach! Surely, he wouldn't go without me would he? Oh was I wrong! We stopped and grabbed a bite to eat on the way to the boarding house from a street vendor. George was soon dressed and heading back out the door, leaving me alone with nothing but my sunburn and thoughts for company. Not being able to sleep a wink, it was in the wee hours of the morning when he finally arrived back to the room. No explanation, no comment, nothing. As I lay there beside him, unable to sleep, it finally sunk home that I was unhappy. This was not the life I had imagined. Did I really know this person I was married to? Vows had been taken, wedding vows that I considered sacred, so who was I to even consider breaking a vow once made? I had made my choice in life, a choice to get away from a controlling father, a choice to get married – albeit to the first person who ever asked me out – and now I had to live with that choice and make the best of it. What on earth had I done!

Our trip back home from the Bahamas was, to say the least, a tad bit subdued. I felt as if a heavy load had settled on my shoulders. Something had changed inside me; maybe all of a sudden, I had grown up and was starting to see things and life in general with clearer vision. Inside I knew I had to just make the best of things; after all, not every marriage was perfect. All that must be done was to focus on the good things in life, to convince myself there were good things.

After arriving back to our little apartment in Vancouver, we returned to work and life resumed its steady pace and routine. Still trying to think of ways to make money, George's next scheme was to play the exchange rate game. Sounded good at first but then, as they say in the gambling world, the bank always wins in the end! So here is what he had in mind. Take a few hundred dollars – garnered from a cash advance on a credit card – exchange the Canadian dollars for American dollars in Canada then cross the border and exchange the American dollars back to Canadian dollars when the exchange rate went up in America. Now this might sound like a good plan on the surface since at that time you received more money for a Canadian dollar than an American dollar when you crossed the border, but there was a catch. Remember, the bank always wins? Each time you exchange money, whether it be in a bank or at a grocery shop, a commission is taken out of the transaction. In fact, going to a bank was much preferable to crossing the border and just exchanging your dollars at a grocery shop since a lot of places at that time exchanged American for Canadian dollar "at par," or one for one. In my mind I just knew this was not going to work! It was a huge gamble. When it came time to exchange the money, the exchange rate might have gone up instead of down and with our luck, the type of dollars we held – Canadian or American – would be on the losing end of the scale! I tried to point this out but to no avail. After all I was told, I was no math whiz!

Have you ever been in a situation where you so badly want to say, "I told you so!" but you bit your tongue and kept quiet because you were afraid of the consequences? That sort of sums up the exchange rate debacle! Needless to say, it was not at all a money-making proposition!

George had a number of fellow bus driving friends who lived in the downtown area of Vancouver, most within walking distance of our apartment block on Haro Street. One very good friend of his, Phil L., lived just a couple of blocks away. He was a good few years older than George, a confirmed bachelor and superb cook. We frequently met up at a little café for a cup of coffee and a sweet bun, occasionally going over to Phil's apartment for a delicious meal.

One day, as George and I were walking down neighbouring Robson Street where we did a lot of our grocery shopping, we saw Phil and a young gentleman coming out of a shop farther down the road. They didn't notice us at first as they strolled along hand in hand. Now seeing two gentlemen holding hands in downtown Vancouver was not exactly uncommon. What was surprising was seeing Phil doing this! Looking up, Phil saw us, immediately dropping his young friend's hand, his face turning beet red. George, a very stony look of disapproval on his face, began to walk right on by.

"Hello Phil!" I said, stopped and greeting our friend as if nothing untoward had happened.

"Hi Rose! Hi George!" Phil replied giving me a grateful look. "This is my friend Pete," introducing us to his friend.

"Good to meet you, Pete." I said, reaching out to shake the young man's hand. After a few minutes awkward silence, I took George's hand, saying, "Well, see you later! We have shopping to get on with." Then we continued on our separate ways.

I could not understand why George was so upset. After all, had we not wondered if Phil might have tendencies towards gentlemen rather than ladies? Surely this should not change our friendship with him, should it? In the long run it did not. I think Phil felt relieved that "his secret," as he called it, was finally out in the open. We resumed our occasional dinners at his home and he remained a good friend. In fact, I was soon to greatly appreciate Phil's friendship more than I could have ever imagined.

Chapter 7.

Funny how life can be so full of surprises. The road you travel, far from being smooth, is filled with ups and downs, twists and turns. Here I was, 22 years old and three years into married life, living not out in the country surrounded by animals, but in a high-rise apartment building in downtown Vancouver, B.C.

I had changed in those three years. Not that I myself noticed the transformation, but others did. One day, my dearest friend Kim and her husband Rob made the trip down from northern Canada to visit us for a couple of days. It was an interesting visit. I could tell Kim, normally a very outspoken young lady, had something on her mind she was not sharing with me. It was a long time before she shared her thoughts with me about that visit, finally letting me know what a different person I had become after marrying George.

Years later, after I had married my dearest Darrell, I sent her a photograph of me fishing. In a letter dated October 20, 1987, she wrote, "Your fishing picture is very interesting. Do you realize it is almost a complete reversal back to when we were about 18? This is the Rose I have always known and loved and what my mental picture of you has always been. You did an excellent cool, sophisticated and suave when you were with George, but I realized you weren't comfortable in that image. To be completely honest, you were getting so "together" that I began feeling uneasy, because I couldn't match your new standards. You weren't giggling anymore. You were not you." Those words Kim wrote were so telling of how much I had changed from the girl she went to school with in Fort Nelson years ago… but here I am, getting a little ahead of the story.

When George and I were first married, we would often talk about having a family. Growing up as an only child more or less – my stepsister Sarah only being an occasional part of my life, more is the pity – I wanted to have children. Lots of children! At first, it made sense to me when George said we should wait until we were more settled and could move down to the little house in Tumelo. After all, Vancouver was no place to start a family. Yet it was hard not to yearn for a child of my own, especially when we learned his sister Becky was expecting. Hard to see other people I knew or even total strangers on the street, their bellies showing they were soon to be new mothers. Then the day arrived when I began to suspect I myself was with child. Could it really be? Secretly, I hoped it was so. My monthly time went by, my skirts seemed to be fitting a wee bit more snugly than usual around the waistband, could I possibly really be pregnant?

Our doctor at that time was an older gentleman whose office was located downtown on Granville Street in an old, somewhat run-down building. Dr. White, aptly named, as his hair was white as snow, ran a clinic that seemed to cater to all manner of people. The waiting room was usually busy, the numerous ashtrays dotted about the room filled to overflowing and a perpetual haze of smoke filled the air. George insisted he was a good doctor, and I must admit, he was a kindly old gentleman, reminding you of a somewhat down in the heel Father Christmas!

As a few more weeks went by with no sign of my usual monthly courses, I decided I had better make an appointment with Doctor White. It would be easy to pop down to his clinic during one of my lunch breaks as I just had to see if I was in the family way. A simple test confirmed I was indeed expecting.

My heart soared! I think I must have walked back to work
with a big grin on my face! No longer did I mind the tight-
ness of my waistbands, no longer did I wonder why I often
felt queasy in the mornings. Throughout the day I would
find myself gently touching my belly and marveling there
was a child growing inside me. At lunchtime I would pick
away at food, sometimes feeling hungry yet, when I started
to eat, feeling a wee bit nauseous yet delighted to feel so!
I was not at all sure why I had not yet broken the news to
George, for he had to be told sooner rather than later. He
would be so happy I thought, even though it was not in
our plans to start a family right now, how could he not be
as thrilled as I was? Since he was back working night shift,
I would catch his bus later that evening and tell him the
good news.

Dashing home, changing clothes and quickly making a
sandwich for George and one for me, I headed off to
catch his bus. It was getting dark; most people had already
headed home so the bus was comparatively empty. Soon,
we were nearing the end of his route where the bus would
sit for a good half an hour before heading back on its loop
into the city. This was when the last of the passengers
would disembark and we could talk without interruption.
Why was I feeling so nervous all of a sudden? This was
good news I had to share. I could imagine how happy he
would be, how he would hug me and make me feel he
truly was delighted a baby was on the way. So, why oh why
was I so uneasy?

"I have some good news to tell you George." I said, not
looking at him, eyes down on my sandwich.
"Oh? What sort of news?" he said as he munched away.
"I am expecting a baby." Now I looked at him, waiting to
see the smile cross his face, waiting to see that look of
wonder and joy to hear he was to be a father. It did not

come. Instead, there was a moment of silence before the words that would forever be seared into my brain left his mouth.

"Well, you will just have to get rid of it." My heart dropped, tears filled my eyes, and I felt sick, really sick to my stomach. This was not an unwanted puppy we were talking about here. This was a baby, our baby, something miraculous! No, no, no, he could not have meant it!

"What do you mean? What are you saying? I can't believe you are saying that! I thought you wanted children!" My mind was in a whirl, I could not catch my breath, feeling as if the whole world was tipping upside down. I would not, absolutely could not get rid of this baby. My body was changing; I could feel my belly swelling, feel the need to nurture this new little life inside me.

"We can't think of starting a family right now, you know that! We're not ready, it's just not the right time." Was he really saying this to me?

"You just need to see Dr. White and he will help you get rid of it." He said with finality.

"It!" He calls our baby "It" No, I thought to myself, there was no way I was not going to have this baby. Fierceness seemed to fill me as I sat there in the silence that surrounded us as the bus began its journey back into the city. Neither one of us spoke as I got off at the stop closest to our apartment building. Walking the short distance home in the dark, my mind was made up. I would leave George. I would never, ever give up this child!

The next few days were so very hard to get through. Waking up in the morning, getting ready for work, leaving home without a word to George, walking the 10 blocks to the Pacific Center. Opening up the little shop and plastering a smile on my face when all I wanted to do was curl up in a ball and cry. Feeling sick inside as I tried to figure out what to do. Could I live on my own? Could I manage? I had never been on my own in my life! Somehow, I would make it, I had to make it! Yes, I convinced myself, yes, I can do this!

Barely a word passed between George and me over the next few days and a frosty silence seemed to pervade the apartment when we were in it together. He changed shift and was now working days, which meant we were together at night. Once away from the shop and customers, I let my sadness and anxiety fill me. Tears came at unexpected moments, and I let them flow. One night, we had a right old row.
"There is no way I am going to lose this baby!" I told George. "If it means I have to move out then that is what I will do."
It hurt me to the core when he said,
"You need to do what you think you need to do. If you want to move out, go ahead. That's fine with me, go ahead and leave." I felt lost. Maybe it was the row, maybe it was all the stress of arguing, of knowing I was going to have to make it on my own that brought on the agonizing cramps in the middle of the night.

I had never felt such pain before; pain that made me cry out … then I felt the warmth between my legs. Getting out of bed, my nightgown was bloody, I felt dizzy and sick as I fell to my knees. George, pale-faced, called Dr. White who told him to take me straight away to the emergency room at the hospital. The miscarriage left me feeling devastated. Surprisingly, Dr. White told us it was not at all an uncommon occurrence when he checked me over a few days later. George was by my side, solicitous and caring. Holding my hand and telling me everything would be all right. I could not bring myself to share what had happened with those I knew, not even Cornelia, so we decided to keep it quiet and just say a touch of appendicitis had kept me off work for a few days.

Life seemed to return to a semblance of normal in many ways, yet things had changed, drastically changed. I was depressed, cried at the drop of a hat, felt as if there was something wrong with me, that it was my fault I had lost the baby. How easy it was to blame myself. One night, feeling as if the whole world was against me, I climbed up on the edge of our balcony railing; looking down onto the street below, ready to fall into oblivion. Such was my state of mind that the thought of suicide was welcome. Then, as I prepared to go over the edge, a small voice intruded, a silly voice of reason.

"You don't really want to do this you know." it said, "You are no good at anything! Okay, so you are 12 floors up, but with your luck you'll miss the pavement and land in the Rhododendron bushes and be maimed for life instead of killed!"

Tears flooded my eyes, that little voice in my mind was right; I was no good at anything and was bound to mess this up too! I climbed down and sank in a heap on the balcony floor, sobbing my eyes out. George, either unaware of what I had contemplated or totally unconcerned, impassively continued to watch television. Once again, the thought was there, creeping into the forefront of my mind... "Oh Rose, what have you done?"

Chapter 8.

Life, what a journey! It was not all bad you know, there were good times too such as when we would take holidays and travel. Like the trip to Disney World's Epcot Center where I guess the little girl still inside of me reveled in the rides and fantasyland. Becky, my sister-in-law, was my idol. Married to a dentist in Waco, Texas, she epitomized the perfect wife and mother. Although barely older than me, she seemed so "together" in her life, an immaculate house, a devoted husband and a lovely person inside and out. To Becky, I told all. When we went down to Texas in early 1984, I think she saw a change in me. Before I knew it, all my woes were laid in front of her and I found a staunch, compassionate friend. Becky and I had always got along well together, but sharing news of my pregnancy, miscarriage and most of all, her brother's response to my being pregnant, made us closer still. In her I found a warm, understanding shoulder to lean on. She made me feel things would all work out for the better in the end.
"George is a different sort of person and always had been. He just needs a bit more time to get his life in order." she said. "Just give him time."

It really is amazing how a person can adjust and adapt to things. I came to realize that my married life was not the perfect bed of roses that I thought it would be. I also came to see that one could manage and make the best of things if one had the right attitude. More and more George started talking about moving to the states and into the little house on the acreage in Tumelo. Although we never openly discussed it, I assumed this meant starting a family. There was, however, a big stumbling block to overcome, namely my father and the money we – namely George – had borrowed.

I did not have a bank account of my own, nor was I a joint account holder with George. My and his wages were deposited in the bank and his was the only name on the account and cheque book. Since he took care of all the bills, I assumed payments were regularly made to my father. Did I ever question this arrangement? Of course not! We lived within a strict budget whereby I was given money each month for groceries and other sundry supplies, although was allotted money for clothes, shoes and such too. Compared to when I lived with my father, I felt comparatively rich!

As the idea of moving south kept percolating in George's mind, something else was percolating too. An idea that, when presented to me, appalled, shocked and scared me something terrible! George wanted to renege on paying my father back the money we had borrowed – I say we since my name was also on the promissory note despite it being fully George's idea! The thought of doing such a thing terrified me. Now it was true in the past few months' things had once again slipped into the sour side when it came to relationships with my father, finally culminating in a very stressful and heart wrenching confrontation one evening right there on Haro Street.

George's workday was over before mine, so he often would meet up with me as I came out of the Pacific Center after locking up the little shop for the night. As we headed home in the rain, walking the 10 blocks down Haro Street – which was a lot quieter traffic wise than the bustling Robson Street one block over – I noticed my father's car coming towards us. This was odd, because my father and I were not exactly on speaking terms right then. At first, I thought he might want to remedy the rift, which would have made me happy as I hated being on the outs with him. George wanted to keep walking as my father pulled up alongside us. I however stopped as my father rolled down his window and beckoned me over.

"Hello Daddy," I said as came up to the side of the car. Why did I always feel nervous when I saw him? Always feeling like a little girl who had done something naughty.

"Hello Rose. Why don't you get in and I'll drive you home?" I looked towards George and knew this was not going to be an option and I think my father realized this too as he crossly said,
"I told you to get in the car!" He reached across the seat, undoing the latch on the passenger door, swinging it wide.
"I can't right now. George wants us to walk home." I replied, casting another look in George's direction.
"You need to make a choice right now, Rose. Time to choose between him or me! I'm your daddy!" I stepped back in shock. How could he ask such a thing? Make me choose between him and my husband? Inside me I knew there was no possible way I could go back to living with my father, not after having been away for the past few years. Besides, I was married, I had taken sacred vows and there was no way I could walk away from that!

"Don't ask me to choose such a thing! Please don't! I'm married now. My life is with George. I am staying with him!" I stepped back away from the car to where George waited for me. My father's face held a mixture of sadness and anger. It frightened me, but my place was with my husband. Turning resolutely away from the car, George by my side, we walked on towards home, never looking back. I was too afraid to look back, afraid of what I would see on my father's face.

Was this to be the catalyst that made what was to come next in our life? Maybe. For it was not too long after this incident on Haro Street that George began looking into bankruptcy laws in both Canada and the United States. Bankruptcy? Surely, we were not so badly off that we had

to resort to such a step as that were we? No, we were not.
The reason was made perfectly clear to me one afternoon.
We were going to default on the loan to my father. This
scared me more than the confrontation with my father on
the street had. George must be mad to even consider such
a thing! Surely he knew what my father was like by now?
This was not only morally wrong, but pure madness.

George's idea was to make it appear as if we were bor-
derline destitute. For example, he planned on charging
as much as could up things on his credit card to show we
owed money. We would surreptitiously make a trip to Texas with most of his possessions that were worth anything,
storing them at his parent's house for safekeeping. It was
also a good time to make plans for the move to Oregon.
This meant obtaining an immigrant visa for me, since at
that time, being married to an American citizen no longer
gave one automatic immigrant status in the States. The nice
Volvo car was sold and replaced with a rather beat up 1973
Volkswagen Super Beetle. At this time, with the exception
of one or two close friends, no one had any idea of our
plans. George absolutely did not want to take a chance of
my father finding out what we intended to do! If all went
well, we would move to Oregon early in 1985. I could see
so many flaws in this plan. I loathed the idea of cheating
my father out of his money, which went totally against all
my principles. It was wrong, just plain wrong, but who was
I to try to change my husband's mind.

Late in the year, the visa process for me was started at the
American Embassy. George, being a United States citizen
did not have to do anything of course, but the paperwork
for me was daunting! The number of forms to be filled out
seemed never ending. Affidavits were signed and nota-
rized, background checks completed and person-to-person
interviews begun. During this time, George made several

trips, by himself, down to Central Oregon. I was under the impression he was working on the little house in Tumalo with the goal of getting it shipshape for when we would move into it at the beginning of the following year. I was so very wrong.

In late November, after giving everyone the impression we were making a jaunt, as usual, to spend Thanksgiving with George's family, we made a final "transfer" trip down to Texas. With the little VW Bug filled to the brim with possessions to be hidden, we would be making a holiday of sorts out of the trip by visiting the great Grand Canyon on our way. Now for those not familiar with these little Volkswagen cars, the engine is in the back, in what would be the boot and under the bonnet – trunk and hood respectively in American vernacular – is the spare tire and storage area. Since it is a little car to start with and I am rather an expert at packing things neat and tidy to save space, it fell to me to cram as much as I could into the car. Thus, the space under the bonnet was jam-packed full to capacity with all manner of bags and boxes.

It was a fun trip in a lot of ways. Heading south from Vancouver, this trip would see us passing through Salt Lake City, down through the canyon lands of Utah to the magnificent Grand Canyon itself. Being as it was outside of the general tourist season, it was wonderful since there were seldom any other sightseers around. The Grand Canyon was magnificent! Words fail to describe the immensity, the grandeur and the intense sense of peace and awe that seeing this special part of America brings to you. We walked along the paths to the overlooks, marveling at the depth of this great chasm. The sun was setting as we finally headed back to the car park. Our sights were set on driving to the town of Flagstaff before calling at a day.

It was dark when we eventually found ourselves not too far
from Flagstaff. Looking forward to the hot meal we would
have before finding a suitable place to park for the night,
as we always slept in the car, we did not expect what happened next! Suddenly, one of the old tires blew out and
the car lurched violently to the side of the road. Getting
out to survey the damage, it was cold, windy, pitch black,
starting to snow and there was not a dwelling in sight. The
spare tire was, of course, well-hidden underneath a pleth-
ora of packages and bags jam packed under the bonnet.
With the aid of a flashlight, everything was unloaded and
stacked at the side of the road and the spare tire removed.
While George worked on changing the flat tire, I began
trying to repack things back into the car. Since he had the
one and only flashlight I was not as careful in my packing
endeavours as I should have been.
"I can't see a thing here!" I grumbled.
"Just hurry up, it's freezing out here." Impatience and frustration laced his voice.
"I'm doing my best, but it's kind of hard to do when you
have the light!"
"Just shut up and get the ****** car packed!" He was
getting angry. Not thinking about what was in one of the
last bags that stubbornly would not squash into the space
I wanted it to, deciding it would by gosh or by golly fit in
that space, I gave the bag a final angry thrust with both
hands.

Pain seared through my right hand. I yelled as I realized
the bag I had so thoughtlessly shoved, contained my butcher knives, one of them, a sharp, thin bladed boning knife.
It had driven itself right through the palm of my hand,
entering that fleshy part between my thumb and forefinger,
just missing bone. Jerking my hand back, I felt blood spurt.
Hastily grabbing a rag, I wrapped the makeshift bandage
around my hand while managing to get the final bag in be-

fore slamming the bonnet closed. Shakily getting into the passenger seat, I said nothing as George wrangled the flat tire into the back behind his seat. Half afraid to look at my hand, as the pain was excruciating.

"How far are we from Flagstaff?" I asked, trying to keep my voice steady.

"Not far. Why? What's wrong?" He could not see me in the darkness but obviously knew something was amiss as we drove off towards our destination.

"I have hurt my hand a bit, that's all." was my reply. Rather an understatement as I could feel the blood dripping down onto the floor mat. "I think I may need a doctor."

"What have you done now?" he asked in exasperation. As I tried to staunch the flow of blood I proceeded to explain about the accident with the bag.

Once in Flagstaff, which was looking rather deserted at that time of night, George found a telephone box and looked up and rang a local doctor. I had no idea why we didn't drive straight to the closest hospital, but never voiced my humble opinion! As it happened, there was a doctor just a short way down the road we were on and he said we could come to his house, which also housed his clinic. Meeting us at the door, he ushered us into his office and commenced inspecting, cleaning and stitching up my wound, telling me I was incredibly lucky no serious damage was done. Somehow, I am not sure he really believed our story of the butcher knife in the bag. Loaded up on pain pills, my hand swathed in bandages, we gave our thanks and headed off down the road where needless to say I spent a very sleepless night. Looking back, I sometimes wonder why we did not go to the local hospital. Maybe it was because they too might not have believed the knife in the bag story!

The rest of the trip was uneventful. Thanksgiving was spent at George's parents' home in Georgetown, Texas. While there, the shiny powder blue paint of the little VW Bug was adorned with splotches of red primer paint from a spray can here and there, making the little car look as if it was in a sorry old state of repair. This, said George with a wink, was to lower its value. Always thinking was George, always thinking. His parents of course, obviously knew of the plan to leave Canada and live in Oregon although nothing was openly said about it – at least not in front of me.

Thanksgiving over, we drove the now empty car back to Vancouver via the shortest route. No sightseeing this time! There was too much to think about and organize as George decided the beginning of May would see us make the clandestine move to Oregon. Yes, May was a good month to move but no one could be told the exact date he emphasized. Not yet, not until just right before we left. Oh, this sounded so familiar. Would I never have the chance to say a proper farewell to the friends I had made over the past few years? Was this going to be another slipping away in the middle of the night episode just like my father would so often do? The grey, wintery skies of Vancouver matched my mood, but little did I know that greyer, sadder days were in store.

Chapter 9.

Do you know how hard it is to know you are going to be leaving a place, but you cannot tell a soul about it? Going to work, bursting to let your co-workers know you are making plans to leave the country yet not being able to say a thing? Talk about stress! Life fell into the same old pattern of work and housekeeping. I had stopped going to the Southland's Riding Club, using the excuse of the winter weather, but it was so hard to give up my Monday riding lessons. That was my special time, time when I let all my cares and worries go out the window. I was tempted to keep up my lessons with Pat just for my sanity, yet what was the point of renewing my annual membership with the club when I would not be here to use it?

After arriving home from our Thanksgiving trip to Texas, another surprise greeted me. One that I met with very mixed feelings, a secret I wanted to keep all to myself. As I felt the familiar changes begin in my body, I began to withdraw into myself, to plan and plot how I could live on my own, survive on my own. For yes, I was sure I was once again carrying a baby! There would be no talk whatsoever of me losing this child. If it meant leaving George and going off on my own, well, that is what I would do. I had a good job, I had friends and convinced myself I could do this! Two of the ladies working in the shop with me, who had been hired on for the Christmas rush, were both expecting a child. They were glowing! My heart ached when their husbands would arrive to escort them home from work, seeing their faces light up with tender joy. Hearing how excited they were to add a child to the family. It made me long to say, "I am expecting too!" yet I kept quiet.

Christmas was not far away when, needing to know for sure, I made an appointment with Dr. White. It was quickly confirmed, I was pregnant. As he held the consulting room door open for me, Dr. White said,

"I will need to run a through more tests, but we can do that later in the week. Has George been told of the pregnancy?" An odd question I thought, accepting the card from him showing the date and time for a follow up appointment.

"No. I wanted to confirm things with you first before I told him." Dr. White seemed surprised when the answer was in the negative.

"Well, take care. See you in a few days."

To my great alarm, and yes, trepidation, there was George, sitting in the waiting room when I arrived at the doctor's office for my next appointment!

"George! What are you doing here?" Had Dr. White called him? He must have. Accompanying me into the consultation office, George sat stoically beside me as Dr. White gave me the devastating news.

"You have a tubal pregnancy, Rose, and as such, it is not a viable pregnancy." I heard Dr. White's words, but they were not sinking in.

"What do you mean? What does that mean!" I began to feel myself falling apart.

"For your own health and safety, the pregnancy must be terminated." Feeling as if I were in a fog, I heard Dr. White say, "An appointment had already been made at the hospital; you will go in right away." Dr. White's next words shattered my heart…

"This is serious Rose, you will never be able to risk becoming pregnant again, you will never be able to carry a child to term."

My world crashed around me. I was numb. George, surprisingly, was incredibly compassionate. I did not question what I had been told by the doctor. I did not question why the doctor had called George. I did not question anything. Oh, how I should have!

My friends, workmates and employer were all under the impression my appendix had flared up again which was why I immediately needed a few days off work. That was George's idea, not mine. The day prior to the procedure George accompanied me to the hospital, the surgeon making him stay in the room while the initial examination took place. I was to be at the hospital the following morning by 6 o'clock, and then should be ready to go home later that same day. A day or two of rest and I was cleared to resume work. My body might be ready for work, but what about my mind? I was in a fog, the depths of despair. How could I pretend I was fine?

Six o'clock the following morning George dropped me off at the entrance to the Vancouver hospital. He had to go he said; he could not stay. Feeling very scared and in pain from the examination the day before, I made my way to the outpatient area, checked in and was prepped for the procedure. I do not recall anything but fear. I was put to sleep, woke up in the recovery room to find not George sitting beside me, but our friend Phil.
"Where is George?" I asked. Phil, taking my hand replied, "He has gone to Oregon. He said he would be staying in Bend for a few days." It was Phil, gentle soul that he was, who took me back to my apartment, brought me hot soup, checked in on me for the three days George was gone. I grieved alone. Cried until there was no more tears left to shed, then curled up in a ball, hands on my empty belly and sobbed even more.

Years later, I was to discover just how far George had gone to ensure I would not have a child. A discovery that shattered me to the core all over again; but this time, I had a

loving, wonderful partner by my side to ease the pain...
but I am getting ahead of myself...

A change came over me. Not a slow change, a leisurely con-
templative change, but a fast, hard eye-opening change. I
might be married, I might be called Rose Ness now instead
of Rose Forster. I certainly had made a huge mistake by not
choosing the Canadian Armed Forces over marriage, but I
was waking up. I would not break my marriage vows, for
they were too sacred. I had made my bed, now I must lie
in it no matter how prickly it was. I would do as I was told,
work, cook, clean, but the rose-coloured glasses had finally
fallen off for good. A shell seemed to have settled around
me, a thick, protective shell.

The New Year came and went. 1985 had begun and with
it the beginning of a new chapter in our lives. This was to
be "Departure Year." Marc and Heidi Singer, Cornelia, who
was now living in Greece, the rest of her family, Phil and a
couple of other friends were finally told we were moving
to Oregon. The date for our departure from Vancouver
was set for May 5th. All that was holding things up was my
visa application. Without a visa, even though I was married to an American citizen, I would not be able to legally
live in the United States. The numerous trips made to the
American Consulate office all ended the same way, in total
frustration. Despite appeals to learn why it was taking so
long to complete the paperwork, we were merely told they
could not give us specific information, other than to say it
was "something" in my father's past that was delaying the
process. No inkling as to what, however. Finally, a few days
before our scheduled plan to leave Vancouver, the visa was
approved.

The rental truck was filled with George's furniture, the
little VW Bug packed with all our clothes when, before day-

light, we began our journey south towards America. Tearful goodbyes with promises to keep in touch had already been made; our new life in Bend awaited. Driving all the way from Vancouver, B.C. to Central Oregon was quite the nerve-wracking experience for me. I had driven around Vancouver quite a bit in the past few months, but this near 500mile journey was something else! George, in the rental truck, led the way while I followed behind in the little car. Stopping only occasionally for a quick bite to eat, petrol refill and bathroom breaks, it was near dark when we finally reached our destination. Feeling disappointed to not be arriving at the cozy little house on the acreage in Tumelo, we pulled into the driveway of a modest house in a cul-de-sac next to many others in the city of Bend. Wearily following George into the dark house, we threw our sleeping bags on the living room floor and promptly fell asleep.

A few weeks earlier, before we left Vancouver, George revealed to me he had sold the Tumelo property and bought a house in the neighbouring city of Bend. There was no explanation why, no discussion, no disclosure of how much the acreage sold for nor the cost of the Pheasant Court house, no picture of what it looked like. This was just where we were going to live, end of story, full stop! The Pheasant Court house was a nice house although very non-descript, blending in with the other houses surrounding it. With a small lawn in front, a large, high wooden privacy fence enclosed the tiny back garden where a few trees shielded the view slightly from the neighbouring houses situated a few feet away on either side. Abruptly gone were my images of a chickens, a horse and country living!

It did not take long at all to move the furniture from the rental truck inside our new home. After living in a 600-square-foot apartment for the past few years the house seemed huge! George had made several trips, by himself I might add, down to Oregon and during one of those trips had made the decision to buy this house. He also, as I was to come to gather, made quite a number of new acquaintances and so felt right at home. I, on the other hand, felt like a stranger. His newfound friends were very nice and polite, but somehow, I just didn't seem to fit in. As they chatted away about skiing, hiking and such, it dawned on me these were activities George must have been partaking in when he came down on those frequent trips to Bend. I was not part of this group; yes, I felt quite out of place.

Bend in 1985 was still a smallish city, very picturesque what with the backdrop of the Cascade Mountains and the clear, blue skies. There was a quaint downtown area filled with small boutique shops, little cafés and a wonderful European pasty shop which brough back memories of home, my English home. The main road running through Bend was Highway 97 where numerous shopping malls and large grocery shops supplied the basic needs of the town. Once I received my new social security card, it was decided I should start looking for a job as George had plans to start his own business. Always fascinated by computers, he had the grand idea of starting a computer repair and custom computer design business.

"This is going to take some time," he said, "and bills need to be paid. It just makes sense you be the one to find a job. Bend's a very touristy sort of town. Finding work as a waitress should be easy enough or try for a position in one of the big department shops!"

So that was that. I was the one who needed to find employment. Work in a shop sounded a lot more appealing to me than being a waitress. After all, I had been manageress of Marc and Heidi's shop in Vancouver and had experience as a shopgirl working in my father's village shops in England. It so happened an advertisement came up in the

newspaper for an assistant manager position in the housewares department at the Bon Marché department shop at
the Bend River Mall. I applied and was given the position.
Working five days a week, alternating between the 9am to
5pm shift and the 1pm to 9pm shift, I became the main
income producer.

Silly me! Here I was, bringing home my pay cheque, handing it over to George, blithely believing that, as he emphatically told me, being a "resident alien," I could not have a
bank account of my own nor be a joint person on his bank
account. My name could not be on our house deed since
I apparently could not own property in the United States
even if I lived here, nor could it be on the title to the cars
parked in the driveway. The little Volkswagen, whom I nicknamed Morris, was my daily driver car while George drove
the newer, shiny sedan he had bought. I was so naïve!
Day in and day out I headed off to work while George
remained at home, working on the computer, building his
business – or so he said.

One day, since we had a fully fenced back garden, I suggested we consider getting a dog.
To my surprise, George was not at all opposed to the idea
and off we went to the local Humane Society pound to
see if we could find a suitable canine companion. Enter
Jasper! Jasper was a two-year-old male Golden Retriever, a
beautiful dog with lots of energy and personality to match!
The card on his kennel door proclaimed he was sent to
the pound because he was a roamer, in other words he ran
off a lot! One of the conditions of adopting a dog from the
pound was that within a certain period of time, the dog
was to be spayed, if a female, or neutered if a male. I had
no problem with that, but George sure did. He felt it was
wrong to, um, remove certain male appendages from a
dog! Quite the argument ensued over the next few weeks

but finally Jasper went to visit the vet and the deed was done! Jasper had never received even the most basic of training but was a smart dog and quickly learned his manners. He had a wonderful temperament, as the breed is well noted for, and was a joy to be around. Since owning numerous dogs in the past, albeit a good while ago, it fell to me to undertake his formal training. Jasper was an easy dog to work with and a very strong bond soon developed between us. He was definitely my dog and I poured love back to him. It was good to have something to love.

Life was slowly moving on, a routine once again settling into place. I had my work at The Bon to keep my mind occupied and George immersed himself into his computer. The folks living in the other houses on the cul-de-sac pretty much kept themselves to themselves, although we were on chatting terms with the very religious family who lived to the right of us. George soon made friends with the single lady who lived on our left although I was sure she was up to something because she belonged to a "Bunco" club. Really? She seemed nice enough to me! It would be years later when I came to discover "bunco" was nothing more than a group of folks, normally women, who got together once a month for a harmless game of dice and a chance to socialize with one another. Not, as George would have me believe, a conspiracy group! Oh yes, I was pretty naïve!

Chapter 10.

1985 came and went. Life assumed a regular routine. I
began to relax a little since there had been no word at all
from my father. He obviously must have no idea where we
were; we had disappeared off the face of the earth as far as
he was concerned, at least that is what I would tell myself.
George and I had what one might call an amicable type of
relationship. We lived in the same house, made trips down
to Texas to visit his family, occasionally went out with some
of his friends; yes, I would call it amicable for the most
part. Occasionally there were upsets such as the time I
found Jasper in the garage, head and shoulders inside the
rubbish bin, tearing into everything with relish!
"Jasper! No!" Without thinking, I picked up the rubbish
bin lid and whopped him with it as such behavior in my
mind was totally unacceptable and he knew it! Wham! Next
thing I knew I was on my knees, my ears ringing, my head
pounding. George had seen me whack Jasper and I guess
he felt I should receive the same treatment! Tears filled my
eyes but not just tears of pain, tears of anger.
"What was that for?" I yelled. I felt like lashing back out
at him, but I did not. Too many years with my father had
taught me to turn my anger inwards at myself instead.
"You hit the dog. There was no need to hit him like that!"
George replied.
"But look at the mess!"
"He's a dog, Rose! Dogs do that! Just get it cleaned up."
Leaving the rubbish laying on the garage floor, the resentment and fury grew inside me as I ran into the kitchen
away from George, culminating in my punching a kitchen
cabinet door with so much force I felt as if I had broken every bone in my hand. George, laughing at me for throwing
such a childish tantrum, did nothing to ease my ire. I had
to do something, I had to find an outlet for all the frustration inside of me, I just had to!

That outlet came, once again, by way of horses. Bend at that time was known for the great number of horses and horse farms scattered through the county. You could not drive far out of the city limits before seeing horses dotting pastures here, there and everywhere. I needed to be around horses – they were a lifeline to sanity for me. My opportunity came in the form of Sally, a coworker of mine who was manageress of the lingerie department at the Bon Marche. Sally was a very striking lady, tall, slender with a mass of Farah Fawcett blond hair and a warm personality to match. We were talking one day in the lunchroom and the subject of horses came up.

"Rose, I know you ride and know horses really well." She said as we sat during our break. "I have a horse which I keep at the Bar-Shoe Ranch, you know, that place between Bend and Redmond. I really need some lessons." I held my breath waiting for her next words. "Do you think you could help me? I would pay you of course." My heart jumped for joy!

"Oh Sally! I would be delighted to help you! Just being around horses would be payment enough! Yes, yes of course! Just say when." It was easy to plan a day and time since our work shifts often coincided. I would meet her out at the barn where her horse was stabled and give her an hour's riding lesson just to be around horses again. With George being so wrapped up in his computer of an evening, I did not think it would be an issue, especially since Sally insisted on paying me some money to cover my petrol expenses. To be around horses again would be pure balm to my soul!

George became acquainted with a couple of chaps who were as infatuated with computers as he was, and the three of them decided to start a business together. Computers were all the rage and ones that could be customized were in high demand. So "Computer Specialists Northwest" was born. At first, the three of them worked out of their respective homes but, as the demand for their services grew, finally opened a small shop in downtown Bend. I guess it was a good arrangement, catering to people who were having computer problems or wanted a custom-built computer made for them. George became more and more occupied with his business, gone all day then secreting himself away in the spare bedroom-cum-computer room at night. For all his diligent work, no money seemed to be coming in from the business.

"George, how is the new business doing?" I asked, leaning against the door frame of his computer room. "You seem to spend a lot of time in here working but you never tell me if it's making money. Is it?" I was feeling brave enough to question him.

"No, we're not making much right now," he said, rather emphatically, "I told you before, it costs so much to start a business it can take a while before any money starts rolling in. Why should you be worried?"

"Well, you never tell me where we stand with the bills."

"Don't worry! You're making enough at The Bon to cover the bills. There's nothing to be nervous about. Now I need to get on with this." He said, turning back to the computer screen. Of course I shouldn't be worried. George had said so! Silly me!

Looking back, this was the time our marriage ultimately started to drift apart. I guess I should have seen it coming, but I didn't. George and I had for quite a while just "lived" with each other and got along for the most part. Is that not what most married couples do? There were disagreements of course, arguments and frustrations on both our parts. Times when I got into trouble for what George considered my unseemly behavior. Such as when we attended a local Amway party one night and I asked the host what George considered very inappropriate questions. I did not think them inappropriate! Here we were, sitting with a group of other couples as the person hosting the party was trying to convince everyone to invest in Amway. A way to make money so fast it will blow you away! Not another get rich quick scheme, I thought.

As we sat there, watching the host and hostess animatedly extoll the virtues of the products they were selling, giving the spiel about how much money a person could make with next to no effort, all I could think of was "If they are making so much money, why are they living where they live, wearing polyester trouser suits still working day jobs for a living, driving an old car and trying to sell us on this idea?" As the presentation concluded, the host asked if anyone had any questions. My hand immediately went up. "So actually, we are working for you selling things while you are working for someone else and they in turn are working for Amway?" I asked. I could feel George looking daggers at me, but I resolutely kept my eyes on the smiling host.

"Well, more or less. But we all make a good living! You would just need to recruit friends of yours and they set up a group of friends too." I could tell my question to him was not welcome! The old adage of "if it sounds too good to be true it probably is" was going through my mind.

"Are we able to see the company balance sheet, or at least your balance sheet?" I asked.

"It seems like a lot of people end up buying an awful lot of product themselves and that would go on their bottom line. So, it is not really a true profit after all, correct?" My simple question was not well received! Other people around me looked in my direction as if I had made a gross faux pas. George was furious with me! After we left and were walking the short distance home, the anger he felt finally erupted.

"How could you embarrass me like that? They made a great presentation!"

"I thought it was a reasonable question. It just seems to be a scam to get other people to make money for them. Do they look prosperous to you?"

"That's the last time I'm letting you come to something like that. You just have no mind for business, do you? You're just too simple, too stupid to learn!" was his last retort. I had been duly told, but it was funny, instead of feeling cowed I felt empowered! I was changing.

As the year came to a close, my solace was being around Sally and her horse. For a couple of hours while at the barn, I could forget life at home, forget my troubles and woes. I felt the gap between George and me growing wider and wider. One evening, we attended a Halloween party at a house down the street, a few blocks away from ours. George had become acquainted with the fellows who lived there and despite a long day at work, I was expected to come along with him. I am not one for parties, never have been and most likely never will be. However, when told to do something I invariably did it.

The party was loud, and in full swing when we arrived. Almost everyone was in fancy dress, although here and there were others in their business suits or casual clothes such as George and I wore. The beer and spirits flowed freely and since I am a near teetotaler, I was content to find a corner with a fizzy pop and sit and watch everyone else behaving rather silly the more inebriated they got! George soon found himself a more agreeable companion than me, a very well-endowed blond-haired lady, dressed in a rather provocative Playboy Bunny costume. It was obvious they were becoming quite enamoured of each other and as it was getting late and I had obviously been forgotten, I thought it would be a good time to head off home. About the time I was trying to catch George's attention, I saw him and the Bunny head towards the big hot tub, already filled with people. Fully clothed, laughing and hand in hand with The Bunny, he jumped right in! I decided I had had enough; I was leaving as I saw nothing funny in the situation! Slipping away unnoticed it was with a heavy heart I walked the dark streets home. It was in the wee hours of the morning when I finally heard the house front door open, and George stumbled in.

It was rather frosty the following morning, both inside as well as outside our house. Something had irrevocably changed between us. I was finally waking up to the fact that our marriage was in shambles and my mind wondered if it could ever be repaired. A shell was forming around my heart.

Not too long after the Halloween Incident – as I thereafter called it – the Christmas shopping rush descended, and work at The Bon kept my mind busy. One day however, I had a right old scare. Genelle, one of my co-workers in the housewares department, said a man had come looking for me while I was on my lunchbreak.

"What man?" I asked her, "What did he look like?"

"Well, he was not too tall, kind of spoke like you do, was older and said he would be back later. Oh, and he left you this" she said, handing me a slip of paper.

My heart pounded. That could be none other than my father. I looked around at the throng of people in the shop, looking for that familiar face as I opened the folded note, immediately recognizing my father's precise handwriting. Five little words struck chords of panic and dread within me, "I know where you live!"

"Are you okay Rose?" I am sure I must have looked ill as Genelle quickly grabbed my arm.

The remainder of the day passed with me constantly scanning the crowds for his face. Walking out after my shift, the winter darkness suddenly seemed menacing. I hurried to Morris, feeling better once I was inside my little car with the doors locked. Arriving home, I was still feeling apprehensive.

"George, I think my father may have found out where we live." I said, hurriedly pulling off my coat, resisting the urge to draw all the house curtains closed. "Or at least he knows we are in Bend."

"Why do you think that?" George asked, "How could he know where we are?" he did not seem as worried as me.

"Aren't you worried about this? I am! My father will never forgive us for leaving in the middle of the night with no word of goodbye, especially because of that promissory note!"

"Don't worry! There is nothing he can do to us down here." George might be trying to sound calm, but even I could tell there was a note of anxiety in his voice.

Each day at work, I found myself jumpy and preoccupied. My conscience was bothering me. Even though I was not the one who wanted to borrow the money, my name was still on that note. I was accountable and my father would not forget that. The tension at home, the anxiety at work of wondering when my father would show up, was taking a toll on me. Thankfully, Christmas season for anyone in the retail business is busy. Last-minute shoppers trying to take advantage of last-minute bargains meant from the start of my workday until the end I actually had little time to dwell too much on life at home. One morning, right before I left for work, my world shattered even more. No emotion in his voice, George's words hit me like a ton of bricks.

"Rose, I really do like you, as a person, but I don't love you anymore." I found myself holding my breath, sure I did not hear the words right. I felt my legs become weak.

"You… you don't love me anymore?" I felt as if all the life
had drained out of me! As he turned and walked away
down the hall, I could not speak. What on earth did that
mean? Did he want me to move out? Get a divorce? What
exactly was I to make of a statement like that? Like an
automaton I left the house, somehow drove to work, my
mind in a whirl. The entire day passed in a fog; I couldn't
concentrate on anything but what George's parting words
had been to me. Words that cut into my heart.

That day seemed never-ending. I was scheduled to work
the 1pm to 9pm shift but as was usual, had come in early. It
was a long, long day, busy with customers but the minutes
and hours seemed to crawl by. I felt I needed to get home,
to sit down and find out exactly what George had meant,
where our lives were heading from here. 9 o'clock rolled
around, the last customers left, the shop doors closed, the
end of day accounting completed and turned in. By half
past nine I was in Morris driving home, my stomach churn-
ing at the thought of the coming conversation. Imagine
my surprise as I pulled into the driveway, walked up to the
front door, putting the key in the lock… to no avail. My
key would not work! The back gate was locked, the garage
door too. Feeling shaky and sick, I hammered on the front
door.

George opened it and stood there.
"My key doesn't work! I couldn't get in." I said, a feeling
of dread stealing over me. He still stood there, barring my
way into the house. "What's wrong George, why can't I
come in?" my heart was pounding. Something was wrong. I
could feel it.
"I changed the locks because someone else is moving in.
You can get some of your clothes for now, but you will
have to find somewhere else to stay tonight and somewhere else to live. I'm sorry Rose." He finally moved aside

so I could enter. Tears filled my eyes, even knowing our marriage was coming apart, nothing had prepared me for this. Not knowing what else to do, in tears I went to the telephone and called my friend Genelle, telling her what had happened. In no time at all she was at the door, her dark eyes staring at George with anger and disdain as she put her arm around my shoulders, took my bag which held a few clothes and led me to her car. I could not have driven, as I could not stop the flow of tears.

Genelle must have known I was in no condition to talk. Making me a bed on her settee, she tucked the blankets around me and just sat there holding my hand. In the morning, we talked over a hot cup of coffee. I opened up and told her everything, my fear of my father, the clandestine move to Bend, everything. She was a sympathetic listener. Assuring me I could stay with her as long as I needed to, she said she would accompany me back to the house, my old house, to pack up more of my things. After calling George to arrange a time to come over, Genelle, true to her word, came with me. Her support was wonderful. With George standing by and Genelle biting her tongue so as not tell him what she thought of him, as quickly as I could, I packed up some clothes and toiletries. A big part of my mind kept saying, "I will be back, I know will be back." The smaller part asked, "Will I?"

Chapter 11.

My whole world changed in an instant. Life had thrown me for a loop, and I did not know which way to turn, feeling tossed around on an emotional sea of disbelief, grief, fear and, yes, a touch of anger. Inside me I knew things had not well been going well between George and me, but no matter what, we had exchanged vows for better or worse. Surely this was just a temporary thing? We would get back together; this was just another bump in the road, wasn't it? Yet an insistent little voice inside me whispered "Oh Rose, you silly girl, he will never take you back!"

So what do I do now I wondered? I couldn't stay at Genelle's place forever; she was married with a life of her own. Of course, word spread, and it was not long before a number of the ladies who worked with me knew of my plight. Sally came up with a plan and emphatically told me she would not take no for an answer!
"Rose, I have a little A-frame house on a small acreage on the road between Bend and Sisters. It is still in the construction stage so nothing much. It would do me a huge favour if you would move in, stay in the place and take care of it for a while for me." My heart leapt and tears came to my eyes at her generosity.
"Oh Sally! Thank you!" I could even have my dog Jasper with me and the old stray ginger tom cat that had recently decided to take up residence at the house in Bend. It sounded too good to be true and I felt so blessed to have such caring and compassionate friends. Now I just had to face George.

After calling him ahead of time to arrange coming over to pick up more of my clothes and with Genelle once again at my side for moral support, George let me know I could take the Volkswagen. Not only that, but he did not want

Jasper or the cat to stay either, so I had better take them. "Whenever you can, but preferably as soon as possible" he called out as I headed down the steps, "you need to come and get all of your other things out of the house too. We can discuss what you can take when you come back," he said, closing the door firmly before I could answer. Genelle and I headed down the garden path. Without my friend beside me I think I would have melted down into a puddle of despair. Those words did not sound as if I would be coming back to stay. Maybe it truly was over, so where do I go from here?

Piling my clothes into the back seat of Morris, I called Jasper from the back garden where he came bounding up to me, tail wagging like mad, eagerly leaping into the front passenger seat. Just having that dog beside me lifted my spirits. Ginger cat was nowhere to be seen; I would get him later I thought as I followed Genelle's car out onto the road. A new adventure was before me, which was how I had to look at this now, yet the tears still ran down my face as I drove away.

The following day after work, Sally took me out to her little house for a look around and to show me where everything was. Set back off the road a short way, a barrier of trees screening the traffic from view, I thought what a delightful place to live! The interior was still in a major state of construction. Unfinished sheetrock on the walls, the floor just bare plywood. Yet it had a little kitchen with running water and a cooker, and for heat, set back in an alcove, was an old wood stove with a pile of chopped wood beside it. A table and old easy chair were the extent of the furnishings other than a small bed upstairs in the loft. It was perfect! Sally had also moved her horse out to the land, so I had an equine companion too. She would accept no rent payments from me, insisting my staying in the house and caring for her horse was payment enough. In fact, we could use her horse trailer to haul whatever other possessions I had yet to get from the house on Pheasant Court. Her friend Herb would even help. I felt so grateful.

When my next day off rolled around, I found myself back in my old house, going through the pile of things George had set aside for me to take. He had boxed up my books and what was left of my clothes, my butcher knives and an old iron of all things! Telling me I could take the pewter, crystal and other odds and ends I had bought while working for Marc and Heidi in the little shop in Vancouver, including William Tell, my beloved carved horse. The meager pile of linens, towels, crockery and such I declined to take, as inside me there was still that little voice saying, "I will be back, I know he will want me back!" Then that other little voice whispered "Really Rose? Are you sure?"
"I have sorted through all our pictures and put the ones I don't want in a box. The furniture is all mine, so I'll be keeping it of course, except for that old chest of drawers; you take that." It was all so cut and dried, so cold and clinical, so well thought out.

Sally and her friend Herb, true to her word, arrived and helped me load up all the packed boxes and bags into her horse trailer, the small pile that now represented all my worldly possessions. Ginger cat was watching the proceedings so before he could wander off again was unceremoniously scooped up and plonked into the car. As Sally and Herb drove away, I turned for one last look at what had been my home. George called me back. In his hand a small package wrapped in bright Christmas paper. Was he giving me a farewell Christmas present? As I reached out to take it, the smile that was forming on my lips died.
"You had better take this with you, it's from Becky. She made us a quilt and this tea cozy for Christmas. I'm keep-

ing the quilt." With that he handed me the package and slowly closed the door. As I heard the lock click into place. it hit me, I was alone, my marriage was over, there was to be no going back.

Christmas was just around the corner. In some ways this was a bit of a blessing as work was nothing but a busy rush from the moment the shop opened until the doors closed at night. It was cold and very snowy that winter in Bend. On Third Street, a four-lane main road running north and south through Bend, the snowplows had piled up excess snow into huge piles in the center of the road, with narrow openings to allow for turning onto side roads and businesses. Since Third Street was also the State highway 97, traffic was a constant flow. Never having driven much in snow before, I was very glad my little car was such a champ, but the drive in from my new abode near Sisters to Bend each day for work was a white knuckle, harrowing ordeal! The defroster in Morris was not very efficient so, every once in a while, I would have to scrape a little hole to see out through the ice buildup on the inside of the windshield. While the window defroster was weak the heater was like a blast furnace on my feet! Yet I loved this little car, it was my little car, my Morris car!

Each day before I headed off to work, Ginger cat would be let out the back door, free to go roaming around the property, doing what cats love to do. Jasper and I would follow, heading off for a long walk. Much to the cat's chagrin, Jasper was allowed to spend the remainder of the day in the house, looking out the big picture window, patiently waiting for me to return. What a grand companion he was for me in a time when I needed something to hold onto and love.

Now Golden Retrievers are not exactly known as great

guard dogs. It seems as if they are the sort that when a
burglar breaks into your home, they bound up to them,
wagging their tail like mad, tongue lolling out the side of
their mouth in a doggy smile. Jasper, however, was different. There was another side to him of which I was glad. He
was the Golden Retriever personality through and through
if he sensed I liked the person I was talking to. If I was a bit
reserved, he would stand firmly at my side, no tail wagging,
no smiling, just alert and watchful with his wise brown
eyes. I had not noticed this tendency in him until there was
just him and me plus Ginger cat as family. So, when in the
middle of the night he leapt off the foot of the bed, flying
down the narrow stairs, growling ferociously then furious-
ly barking at the kitchen door, I knew someone was out
there.

Who could it be? A burglar? George? The unwelcome
thought crossed my mind that surely it could not be my
father! Should I go down and see? Quietly slipping out of
bed, heart pounding, I pulled on my dressing gown and
crept down the stairs to the kitchen where, with one of my
butcher knives in hand, I headed towards the back door.
Jasper by this time had settled down a bit so I turned on
the back porch light and slowly opened the door. Immediately dashing outside, tail held stiffly aloft, Jasper's nose
searching the cold night air for some foreign scent. In the
fresh snow I saw them, the tracks, very fresh tracks, foot-
prints that circled the house. Calling Jasper back inside I
quickly shut and locked the door. The tracks were the size
of a man's shoe, a small man's shoe.My father was a small
man.

Thinking back to the "small man" who had come to where
I worked, asking for me, it was not inconceivable that my
father had indeed found out where I lived. He was a tena-
cious man. Despite my never seeing a penny of the money

George borrowed from him, I knew my father would have been livid after discovering we had slipped out of Vancouver unannounced. I knew, in my heart, one of these days he would approach me and I would have to atone for what had been done. Whether he would believe I had nothing to do with the disappearance of the money or not I couldn't even guess. All I could do is tell my side of the story and hope for the best. I sure did not have the means to pay him back! One thing was certain; I was never going to go back to living with my father. Somehow or other I would make it on my own.

The next few days leading up to Christmas Day were stressful beyond words. Thankfully work was busy so that took my mind off worrying about my situation for the most part. Yet, embarrassingly, out of the blue while serving a customer, I would feel on the brink of breaking down in tears, feeling as if my life were coming apart at the seams. Sometimes, seeing the back of a man resembling my father, the blood would drain from my face and a queasy feeling hit the pit of my stomach. Was it him? Was it my father I just saw? Fear and guilt held me back from calling out or following the person to see. Driving home in the dark, seeing headlights closing in behind me, scared me to death! I did not feel secure until I was in Sally's little house, doors locked with Jasper beside me.

"I can do this. I can do this!" Words said to myself over and over again. I had a job, a place to live, my little car Morris, Jasper and Ginger. Now that I was living on my own I discovered, much to my chagrin, that I could indeed have a bank account! Genelle was amazed when I told her about not having a chequebook or savings account. Listening incredulously when I told her George had insisted as a resident alien I could not have such things in my name. What else could I own that I thought I could not? For starters, a car, a house, the list was endless! Of course, one had to have money for such things and my stock of funds was woefully low; but no worries I reminded myself, "I can do this!"

Chapter 12.

Christmas came and went. New Year's Eve was celebrated alone, just me and my faithful companions Jasper and
Ginger Cat. A new year meant a new start and a new life.
No more evidence was seen of strangers stalking around
the house. Life was settling into a bearable routine. It was
a cold winter, but I was cozy in Sally's little house and so
grateful to have such a friend. A good stockpile of wood
for the woodstove kept me warm, although one night it
almost kept me too warm! I had stoked the fire and banked
it down with a couple big chunks of wood, closing the
dampers so the fire would last through the night. Jasper
and Ginger Cat followed me up the steep stairs to the loft,
immediately finding their preferred sleeping spots on the
bed as soon as I snuggled under the covers.

It must have been a little after midnight when Jasper became very restless, finally jumping down from the end of
the bed and pacing the floor, uncharacteristically whining.
Slowly waking up, I smelled an odd odour, an acrid, burning odour! Fully awake, I ran downstairs to find the unfinished sheetrock wall behind the woodstove blackened
and smoking, near to bursting into flames! The smoke was
quickly filling the room as I opened the front door and
headed for the kitchen. Filling the biggest pan I had with
water, I threw it on the blackened sheetrock in a frantic
attempt to douse the smoking wall. Over and over I flung
water on the wall until it and the surrounding floor was
saturated. The woodstove was still fiercely hot so I did not
dare go back to bed! Sitting wrapped in a blanket with all
the windows and doors open, the chilly winter wind blow-
ing from one end to the other through the house, I waited
for dawn to come. Feeling terrible when I called her to
share the news of the near fire, Sally told me not to worry
about the mess, someone would be over to fix things up.

Come to find out, instead of regular sheetrock, a special fire-retardant board should have been installed behind the stove! Maybe it was a providential thing that the near fire happened when it did and not after the wall had been finished!

Sally's life was changing too, she had a new gentleman friend and had moved from Bend to the small town of Sisters. A little over a month after the near fire, Sally, who had left The Bon, called to say she had decided to sell the little house and land. Someone had come along and made her an offer, which she could not refuse.

"To be honest Rose, I have lost interest in finishing this place. I feel bad asking you to move but I still want to have riding lessons with you. Maybe we can still meet at the Bar-Shoe once a week?" I understood completely and although disappointed, realized this day had to come eventually as she was soon to be married. But now what was I going to do? Living at Sally's rent-free had allowed me to save a little money but it was nowhere near enough to buy a house of my own. Trusting to Fate that something would come up, I started looking for a cheap place to rent.

Was there still a small part of me that kept the hope George might change his mind and let me return to the house on Pheasant Court? Of course there was! Despite the sometimes wishful thinking, deep inside I was honest enough with myself to know that things would never be the same. If I was truly honest with myself, I knew what I had taken for love had been lost a year or so after we were married. It was the thought of being on my own, having to make decisions by myself, not having someone there constantly telling me what to do … that was what scared the daylights out of me! I was a great believer in Fate, wasn't I? Had I not told myself innumerable times that very same thing? Well now I had to live by my words, I must have faith and put my trust in Fate.

Admitting my life with George was over was a hard pill to swallow. After the New Year settled in, we had met and spoken – albeit very briefly – and it was made clear I was no longer a part of his life, he had moved on. He suggested I make the move to file for a divorce. I could have the old Volkswagen car; he would keep the new one. The odds and ends gathered up from the house before moving to Sally's place were mine, he did not want them, nor did he want Jasper. It was so cut and dried. Now I had to make a choice, either head back to Vancouver and resume my old life with my father or pull myself together and make a life of my own.

In the mid to latter part of the 1980s, a lot of people came to the Bend area, or I should say the resort town of Sunriver on the outskirts of Bend, to purchase second homes. Vacation homes they called them, which they might only visit a couple times during the year. Many of these newcomers came into The Bon to equip these homes with sundry supplies from towels to sheets, to kitchenware and electronics. One day as I was assisting a tall, well-tanned lady, sure she was one of the frequent "second homers" as we called them, the subject of horses came up.
"We have a farm on the east side of Bend where I raise Trakehners" she said. Since I had ridden a number of that breed of horse, I was very familiar with them.
"Are they Polish or German?" I asked.
"You're familiar with Trakehners? Most people I talk to don't even know what they are!" she replied in amazement. "I have imported some mares and a stallion from Poland. You must come out to the farm. Let me give you directions." With a smile she added, "I am looking for a new barn manager too by the way. When you come out we will talk." Excited to go and see what promised to be some

gorgeous horses, I arranged to visit on my next day off. The lady's name was Joyce Pedigo and she was owner of Eagle Point Trakehners. Was Fate starting to look kindly upon me?

Horses had not entirely left my life when we fled from Vancouver to Bend. Also, through the venue of The Bon's housewares department, I had met an older lady, Alice Loomis. A devotee of dressage and owner of a fine arena and grounds in Bend, she encouraged me to come visit, which of course I did! Just being around her horses was balm to my soul. As well as the regular boarders who stabled their equines with her, she had a trainer in residence, a gentleman by the name of Gary Henley. Gary, a rather taciturn man, was renowned for purchasing off the track thoroughbreds and turning them into spectacular jumping horses. He was apparently in need of an extra groom; not a paid position, but that didn't worry me.

I had eagerly jumped at the offer to be with horses, even if it was just for a couple of hours a day. With George so wrapped up on his computer from the moment he got up until he went to bed, I felt I would hardly be missed! Showing up at the barn well before daylight, I helped feed and groom the horses, tacking them up for Gary to ride then dashing off to work my shift in the housewares department at The Bon. George didn't even seem to care when, on one of my weekly days off work, I would head to the Loomis ranch to be with the horses. When Gary saw my ability to ride, I became the one to pop on the youngsters and cool them down after he had finished schooling them. This became the highlight of my week and my way of keeping some vestige of happiness and sanity in my life.

So here I was, in early 1987, after visiting Joyce's farm and being offered a job, making what I felt was a monumental decision to leave the Bon and go to work for her as her barn manager. My duties would include being in charge of all her horses, the barn staff, riding daily, training youngsters and caring for the broodmares. For this, I would be paid a monthly salary as well as have a beautiful, fully furnished house at my disposal. It was a dream job! My time at Eagle Point Trakehners was wonderful. The facilities were spectacular and the horses top quality. I got along well with the other ladies who worked there and soon started giving riding lessons to some of the folks who boarded at the facility. Joyce's stallion, Adler, was in training down in California with Gwen Stockebrand, a very well-renowned dressage rider and instructor. On occasion he was shipped to Oregon in order to fulfill his studly duties with some of the farm's mares. One such time, Gwen accompanied Adler to Oregon where she gave a dressage clinic which I organized and was able to participate in. It was an upper-level dressage clinic and how much I learned from her over those few days!

I could have stayed at this dream job for years, had it not been for the fact that Joyce was a wee bit of a fickle horse owner and employer. There were a number of young horses between the ages of yearlings to three-year-olds we had been conditioning and working, that Joyce had advertised for sale. One of my duties was to field the telephone calls that came in from prospective buyers from around the country. On numerous occasions, Joyce made arrangements for buyers to come and see her horses. One couple she had spoken with extensively flew in from Florida. Joyce had actually made a commitment to sell a young horse to them and they were arriving to finalize the sale. The youngster was prepared for the viewing, which went very well indeed, but, to the consternation of the prospective buyers, Joyce decided at the very last minute she wished to keep the horse. This willy-nilly approach to showing and selling – or not selling – her horses was so stressful, both on me and all the ladies who worked there, that I decided to hand in my notice.

It was a very difficult decision to make; yet I felt it was the right one for me. I guess I did not have a tough enough shell when complaints from prospective buyers started coming in! There was a young up and coming dressage trainer in the area, Kathy Casey, and I recommended her to Joyce as my possible replacement to work with the horses. We parted on good terms and that was what was most important to me. It was hard leaving my equine pals, horses I had come to love, but I knew it was time. I was ready for the next adventure in my life.

Fate once again took hold of my hand. Some of the boarders at the farm decided it was also time to leave Eagle Point Trakehners and I was approached by three of them, asking if I would be interested in working with their horses as well as continuing to give them riding lessons. Yes, indeed I would! Thus began my fledgling business as travelling riding instructor and horse trainer. At that time in the Bend area, although there were a large number of riding instructors, none would travel to teach at a client's home. Those who wanted lessons either had to board at the instructor's stable or trailer to whatever establishment the instructor taught at. It was not long before I found myself busy and earning a modest living, filling a niche and doing what I loved. With Jasper sitting the in the passenger seat beside me, my saddle, bridle and other tools of the trade in the back seat, my little Morris was soon to be seen travelling all over Central Oregon.

One of my biggest challenges, and yes, I must admit, fears when I left Joyce's farm, had been finding a place to live. Here I had gone from being a wife and living in a relatively nice house in Bend to moving into a partially finished cabin, courtesy of a friend, followed by residing in a beautiful little home on the Trakehner farm… now what? Once again, things fell into place and miraculously worked out. But I am getting ahead of myself again.

When I began giving Sally riding lessons while we both were still working at The Bon, her gentleman friend at the time was a crusty older fellow by the name of Herb. He lived in an ancient, rough looking, small singlewide trailer by the railroad tracks on the property behind the Bar-Shoe riding arena. Situated on the highway between Bend and Redmond, the Bar-Shoe consisted of acres of undeveloped land, a large, somewhat dilapidated covered riding arena, as well as an adjoining stable row where several people boarded their horses. This is where Sally had kept her horse for a while and was the perfect place for us to continue meeting for lessons.

Herb, having a strong affection for the spotted Appaloosa breed, owned a stout horse by the name of Kid. He was always around when Sally had her riding lessons, but seldom had much to say, preferring to just sit and watch, his cowboy hat pulled down low over his eyes. When Sally came to help move my meager possessions out of the Pheasant Court house, it was Herb who had come along with her. He was a building contractor by trade. Now Herb, as I say, loved Appaloosa horses. One day, after attending the livestock auction in the neighbouring town of Madras, he came home with a feisty, short in stature, very spotted Appaloosa horse. It had been sent to the auction sale, to be sold for slaughter, due to his history of running away – seriously running away – with anyone who tried to ride him.

It was chilly in the barn that night. Sally's lesson had ended and while she untacked and groomed her horse. While

getting ready to head back to Sister's, I sat with my hands wrapped around a steaming cup of coffee, trying to warm up before my trek home to the Trakehner farm. Herb, sitting beside me asked,
"How is Sally doing with her horse?"
"Really well!" I replied, "She is a natural rider, one of those long-legged ladies that just seems to drape herself on a horse. I do hope she keeps on riding."

"Come look at this little pony I picked up at the sale yard the other day," he said, getting up and gesturing down the stable aisle. Cup in hand I followed as he headed down the stable row to a stall near the end.
"What do you think of him?" he asked as I peered into the dimly lit stable. There stood a wide-eyed, very – and I mean very – spotted Appaloosa horse.

White, with a multitude of chestnut-coloured spots, standing just tall enough to be considered a horse instead of a pony, he stood in the far corner eyeing us humans with suspicion. Unlike the majority of the breed, this fellow had a thick unruly mane and a flowing tail. Speaking softly, I entered the stable and walked in to say hello, stopping just a few feet from him. After stretching his neck out and tentatively sniffing my extended hand, he snuffled and came towards me for a scratch. Little did I know I had found an equine partner that would help fill a void in my life just when I needed it most.

Watching as the little horse followed me to the stable door as I turned to leave, Herb said,
"How would you like to take him on as a project for me? See what you can do with him."
"Really? I would love to, but I don't know if I could keep him out at Joyce's farm. I honestly do not know how long I will be there" I replied. Sally already knew my dilemma with the vagaries of my current employer and that

I might soon be moving on and I was pretty sure she must have passed this information along to Herb. After all, they were still close friends!

"Well, I can keep him here with Kid and you can ride him whenever you make it out. Do with him what you want; I'll take care of the costs" Herb said. How could I turn that down! A horse to ride, one I could consider like my own, something to settle my mind when I was filled with doubts about my future.

"Okay! I will do it. Thanks Herb!" I felt elated, my first horse in training!

Maybe I could make a living on my own I thought as I got in my little car with faithful Jasper by my side. Driving back to Bend, I felt I was ready to make another big step forward in my life. Yes, hard as it would be, I would talk to Joyce and hand in my resignation. Now decision making has never been my forte, yet it seems once I actually do make a decision, right or wrong, I am at peace with it. This felt like the right decision. Terrifying, but right. Now all I had to worry about was what on earth was I going to do about a place to live!

Chapter 13.

The following morning, I was somewhat surprised that
my resolve to resign was still firm in my mind. Heading to
the barn for early morning feeding chores, always the first
one out there, I was greeted by the nickering voices of the
horses that had become dear to me. Koralka, with her colt
by her side, resided in the first large stable. As a stroked
her soft muzzle and scratched Kourageous behind his ears,
I remembered the night I helped bring him into the world.
Next to Koralka was Werwa – pronounced Verva – a giant of
a mare who had a special place in my heart.

She was a fickle mare. Standing close to 18 hands high,
she had developed a frustrating habit of raising her head
as high as she could so as to avoid being haltered unless
a tasty tidbit was offered! Now I did not believe a horse
should be training the humans and this was exactly what
Werwa was doing! Dictating the terms of when she should
go out to the pasture, when she should be brought in –
she hated being caught – and doing her best to dominate
any human who came in her stable. That did not sit well
with me at all! One of my first encounters with Werwa still
makes me smile.

None of the ladies who worked as stable hands at the farm
liked to bring the mare out for her daily grooming and
turn out. She was big, bossy and just plain spoilt rotten!
Deciding this had to change, I went into her stable with
halter in hand, not hidden behind my back like the other
ladies would do, but in plain sight. I also had an empty
five-gallon bucket with me. All the stables in Joyce's barn
were oversized and well appointed, giving ample room
and comfort to their equine occupants. Thus it was easy
for Werwa to circle me as I stood calmly in the center of
the stable, ignoring her completely. After a short while, not

understanding why this human was not playing her game and trying to catch her, she came over and stood in front of me. Stroking her nose I turned and left. A few minutes later I came back, bucket and halter in plain sight and the whole circling thing started again, but only for a couple of circuits. Once again, she came and stood in front of me.

This time, I upturned the bucket, stood on it and calmly slipped the halter on her head, buckling it securely. Werwa immediately reared back, lifting her head has high as it would go, but she did not count on me having a very firm hold with both hands on the noseband of the halter. Finding herself with a human stubbornly hanging on to her, she tried to raise and keep her head high, but to no avail. Determined not to let go until the mare dropped her head, my feet dangling in the air, it was a battle of wills that was surprisingly short lived. Pretty soon my feet were back on the ground, Werwa's head relaxed and the halter soft in my hands. I let go, patting and praising her for being such a good girl. Slipping the halter off her now lowered head, I patted her neck one more time and left the stall, much to her bewilderment!

Once again, I gave her a few minutes to contemplate this strange turn of events. Upon entering her stall for the third time, she promptly walked up, lowering her head while I slipped the halter on and buckled it up. Meekly walking by my side, she left her stable a perfect lady and stood stock still for her morning grooming session. Werwa and I from that day onwards became partners and friends. She was a delight to ride; something I discovered had never been done since she was imported to America from Europe. Towering over me, a powerhouse of a mare, she was actually a gentle giant. Oh, I would so miss this horse.

Was I sure about leaving? Confident that I could make it

out in the wide world all on my own? No, I certainly was not. Maybe I was wrong to even think about giving up what I had here on Joyce's farm. I was more or less my own boss, surrounded by beautiful horses and living in a lovely little house. With a steady wage coming in and no bills to pay except for petrol and groceries, I was living a dream. Yet here I was, contemplating giving it all up just because I did not particularly like my employer's way of handling her horses. What was wrong with me? Maybe I was more like my father than I thought; maybe I had inherited those itchy feet of his, that compulsion to always be on the move. No, it was more than that I decided. I was following my heart and inside me, knew I was doing the right thing.

But where on earth was I going to live? I still did not have that much money saved up and the thought of finding a place to live was a wee bit daunting. I had no credit at all and most rental places wanted to see a solid credit history. Somehow, prospective landlords did not feel it was in their best interest when you told them you always paid for everything in cash. Brought up with the mantra that if you do not have the money to pay for something then you cannot afford it, made the idea of buying on credit somewhat abhorrent. Then there was the fact that in order to get credit you have to have had credit! So when I went to apply for my first credit card I was turned down because I did not owe anyone any money! Now that made a lot of sense!

Joyce took my resignation in stride. I gave her my recommendation for a replacement manager and left on good terms. Apparently frequently changing staff at the farm was a common occurrence, as I discovered shortly after I left. When I departed, so did three of the other ladies, deciding they too wanted less stress and drama in their lives!

I was now ready to begin the next chapter in my life as a

travelling riding instructor and horse trainer. Chatting with Sally and Herb one evening at the Bar Shoe after Sally's lesson, just before I left Eagle Point Trakehners, I was lamenting the fact of how daunting it was trying to find a place to rent. One where Jasper and Ginger Cat could be with me. Most landlords required substantial upfront money for first and last month's rent plus security deposits, but I was finding they certainly did not want someone with a dog and a cat. There was no way I was getting rid of Jasper and Ginger Cat; I would live in Morris before I did that!

"If only you still had your little house, Sally." I jokingly said, "I would be a grand renter, the best you could ask for!"

"I sometimes wish I still had that place." She replied. "I should never have sold it although I can't imagine living in it." We chuckled as we remembered the night it could have burned down that cold, cold night at the turn of the year. Herb had a thoughtful look on his face as he sat there listening to us.

"You could always move in here. Move to the Bar-Shoe." He said quietly. "I'm going to be moving to Bend. A friend of mine has a big house, too much house for one person, so I'm going to live there. That would leave the old trailer empty."

"Are you serious? Do you think the owners would rent to me?"

"Sure! As long as they get paid each month, they won't care who rents the place. In fact, you just pay me and I will pay them. I'll tell them you're 'sub-renting' the place from me."

Oh, this was perfect! A reasonable, well actually dead cheap rental, where I could keep Jasper and Ginger Cat, what more could I ask for. The old trailer was not much to look at, it was right by the railroad tracks, but it would be mine. Since I had prospective clients in Bend and Redmond, the Bar-Shoe, being smack between the two towns, would be an ideal place for me. A smile lit up my face; Fate was smiling upon me too.

Yes indeed, the hand of Fate was leading me forward, carving a path through the tangle of vines that had once threatened to bind and hamper me. Life is full of surprises, twists and turns and challenges that often test your mettle. Yet Fate always has a plan. Little did I know that plan was about to be revealed. My life was set to change in ways I could never, ever have imagined in my wildest of dreams...

When the road ahead seems narrow, overgrown with clinging brambles, rocky and hard to traverse, to forge ahead can be a daunting task. How much easier it might be to just turn around and head back along the path just travelled, even if it does lead to a return to pain and turmoil. Yet what is that I see in the distance? Is that really a bend coming in the road instead of a dead end as I had thought? Could it be worth trudging on? Am I truly brave enough?

Yes, the way is surely becoming easier to follow! My feet find smoother paths and the clinging brambles are thinning and clutching less and less at my skin and clothes.

Before long, the way opens and brightens to reveal the bend in the road. I cannot see what lies around the turn but how will I ever know unless I look? Squaring my shoulders, eyes focused ahead, I determinedly plod on...

Chapter 14

Funny how life seems to throw twists and turns in your path yet just when you decide to throw in the towel, throw up your hands and give it all up, the way straightens out before you. Smooth tarmac replaces the rutted and bumpy track. Suddenly, you feel as if the way forward is not so daunting after all.

After making the decision to resign my position as barn manager of Eagle Point Trakehners, I had my heart set on building up a small business as a travelling horse trainer and riding instructor. There seemed to be a real need for just such a business. Most trainers either had their own establishment or leased space in someone else's barn, which meant clients had to haul their horses to that location for lessons or board their horses where their trainer worked. My idea was to travel to my client's farm or place where they stabled their horse, giving them individualized lessons tailored directly to themselves and their horse's needs. It worked! Before long I had a growing list of customers.

The move into Herb's little trailer on the Bar-Shoe Ranch was an ideal place for me since it was located between Bend and Redmond, the two main towns where my various clients lived. I easily arranged my schedule so as to teach in Bend on certain days of the week and then Redmond on the remainder. With my saddle, bridle and other horse training equipment piled in the back of my little blue VW bug, Jasper sitting beside me in the passenger seat, we covered a lot of miles in a week. I was not making a ton of money but was at least able to pay my bills. Most of all I was content.

When not trundling around the country giving riding lessons, I spent all my spare time with Herb's little Appaloosa horse, Brumby, as I called him. Apart from giving lessons, I was also doing a fair bit of work with untrained as well as some quite unruly horses with bad habits. Splurging, I bought myself a rather fine Australian saddle. Now I loved my English saddle, but the Australian one gave me a wee bit more security when riding a horse that was determined to unseat me as I could lock myself firmly into the seat! One of those unruly creatures I had to ride was none other than Brumby! He could be more than a wee bit of a handful. His previous owners had sent him to the auction yard because he had the bad habit of running away with his rider. Something that can be quite nerve-wracking to the timid equestrienne! Herb, who had a soft spot for Appaloosas, had bought him, saving him from going to slaughter, then turned him over to me as a "project" horse. "See what you can do with him," Herb had said.

So, I asked myself, what was this little feisty Appaloosa destined for? First, I would have to address the running away issue. My solution to the problem was simple. As a rule, I never wore spurs nor carried a riding whip when working a horse, preferring to use strong legs and a grumpy voice to get my point across. I made an exception, however, with Brumby. The first day we rode out on the open trails that stretched for miles and miles behind the Bar-Shoe, I had riding crop in hand. Initially, he was a perfect gentleman, trotting out nicely, ears flicking back and forth and quite soft in my hands. Then the fun began! His trot became longer and longer, a lovely trot I must say, but as soon as he felt my hands start to gently check his speed, I felt him grab for the bit and we were off to the races! At first I tried all the usual methods of slowing a horse down but to no avail. Ears pinned flat to his head he galloped onwards.

It was exhilarating! Since I knew the trail had good footing and went on for a few miles, I decided to just sit tight and enjoy the ride. Leaning forward I grabbed a handful of his mane and let him go. After a while, puzzled no doubt that his rider was not hauling on his mouth in a vain attempt to slow him down, I felt his momentum slacken, his speed diminish. Slowly he went from a gallop to a nice canter, then as he slowed down to a trot he got what I had been waiting for.

"Oh no, laddie, no stopping yet! On you go!" I called as my legs squeezed his sides. In surprise, he sped up a little but then once again wanted to drop down to a trot. One swift thwack with the riding crop and he was off again. I asked him gently to slow down and he refused. No worries I thought, there was still good trails ahead of us. When he did start to slow down on his own, my legs and another whack of the crop had him galloping forward yet again.

This happened three more times. Finally, a gentle squeeze on the reins saw him slowing down, softly responding to my hands.

"Easy laddie! That's a good boy, easy now!" After bringing him down to a walk, letting him cool down and think about things, I squeezed my legs and encouraged him forward into a nice gentlemanly canter. Allowing him more rein, his ears started to pin back, and his pace began picking up but just a gentle closing of my hands and a soft "Easy now laddie!" brought him immediately back under control and down to a gentle trot. We had come to an understanding.

The next few days were wonderful! My lesson had sunk in and Brumby never did attempt to run away with me again. What stamina he had! It seemed as if I just couldn't tire him out. What if I were to try him out on a true long-distance ride? For quite a while I had harboured a hankering to try endurance riding. One of the ladies I gave lessons to had an old Arab that in his former life had been an endurance horse. Why not give it a go with Brumby? Of course, since he was not my horse, I would have to run it by Herb first. After all, one would need a truck and horse trailer to get to the races and I had neither.

As it was, Herb was more than willing to go along with my endurance riding aspirations for Brumby once I told him of my plans.

"Sure, I'll haul the pair of you wherever you need to go. You line up the races and I'll get you there," he said. "But we have a problem. The Sanowski's are closing up the barn here on the Bar-Shoe, putting it up for sale. Brumby can't stay here anymore."

"What? Does that mean I will I have to find somewhere else to live as well?" I asked, my heart dropping.

"No, no, you can still live in the trailer for a while, it is just the horse who will need to move. He can come over and be with me and Kid where I'm living. Darrell won't mind an extra horse on the place. It'll mean you have to come over there to ride Brumby, but there are miles of trails back behind his ranch." Herb replied.

Within a few days, plans were made to haul Brumby to his new residence. Although I would be going over there every day to ride, it would be strange not to hear Brumby's nicker of greeting when I came home from a long day of giving lessons. I could already feel myself missing him.

The day of Brumby's move was the first day I met Darrell Howe. Following in Morris behind Herb's truck and horse trailer, we turned off Terry Drive and drove down a white fence-lined gravel driveway that seemed a mile long – it was actually more like a mere half mile as I was later to find out. At the end of the drive was a large and very impressive looking house with a barn and shop laying some distance off to the side. Horses grazed contentedly in green fields. For some reason I was nervous. Herb pulled up by the barn, I parked beside him and leaving Jasper in the car, we walked over to where a few people were standing up at the house.

The closer we came to the house, the more it seemed to grow in stature! I was used to large, lavish houses as many of the ladies I gave riding lessons to resided in such establishments, what to me were mansions. The main house of the Pedigo's was a prime example and this house seemed no different. Set on a slight rise, the many large picture windows at the front looked over the green fields that flanked the long, fence-lined driveway. The view certainly was wonderful as the majestic, snowcapped Cascade mountains were spread out in all their glory on the horizon. Several cars and trucks were parked in the driveway, one being an obvious work truck with Darrell's Electric stenciled in green its side. Somehow, as grand as the house was, to me it looked cold and impersonal, not at all my idea of a home. A little log cabin set back away from civilization would suit me just fine compared to the ostentatious house before me. But there, that was just my opinion!

A woman was crouched down, busy planting flowers along the edge of the lawn and stood up as we approached. Nearby a tall, dark-haired man dressed in blue jeans and a denim shirt leaned casually against the frame of the open front door and it was to him that Herb spoke.
    "Hi Darrell! This is Rose. We brought the horse over. She's training him for an endurance horse so will most likely be over here every day to ride." Turning back to me he said, "Rose, this is Darrell. He owns the place."
"Hello," I mumbled, holding out my hand to shake his. Why on earth was I blushing?
"Hi," he replied, taking my hand, "This is Sonja," he said,

indicating the woman who had been planting flowers. She was short, plumpish and very well dressed. As she smiled and held out her hand, she looked every part the type of woman who would hold domain over a house such as the one what lay behind her. Obviously, she must be Darrell's wife, even if he had not introduced her in that way.

Feeling unexpectedly out of place, I was uncomfortable standing there in my dusty riding breeches and boots. Rather like a scullery maid who has stumbled uninvited into her employer's fancy tea-party.

As Sonja stood watching, Darrell walked with Herb and me over to the barn, showing me where Brumby would be staying.
"How about we head out for a ride? You can show Rose where she can take her horse," Herb said to Darrell.
"Sure. Why not," Darrell replied, obviously a man of few words!

After unloading Brumby from the trailer and letting him have a look at his new abode, tying him up inside the barn I gave him a thorough grooming from head to tail. While Herb went to get Kid, Darrell grabbed a halter and headed out into a big field where a group of horses stood near the gate. Catching up a big dun horse, I realized Darrell was leading back to the barn what was obviously a stallion! Although, with arched neck, he eyed spotty little Brumby as he passed by, not a sound came from Darrell's steed. What a well-behaved horse, I thought. Having spent a good bit of time around stallions, I had never seen one so well-mannered as this. As Darrell went for his saddle and bridle, Kook, as he was nicknamed, stood calm and quiet beside us, a perfect gentleman. Indeed, one would not guess he was a stallion by his demeanor.

While Darrell and Herb talked back and forth, I saddled
up Brumby in my English tack. To my surprise and yes,
my astonishment, Darrell merely flicked a few stray bits of
dried grass from Kook's back before throwing his saddle
pad and saddle onto the horse. No brushing or grooming
here! Slipping a hackamore bridle over Kook's head, he
was ready to go. Mounting up, we all rode out towards the
back gate. Darrell's farm, which totaled 80 acres, bordered
what is known as BLM – Bureau of Land Management –
land. There were several hundred acres of this public land
in which to ride, right on Darrell's doorstep. The sandy
ground was outstanding footing for galloping on, the occasional downed juniper tree a natural jump. As we rode
along, I could see what fun I would have riding Brumby
down these trails each day. A perfect training ground for
his first competitive endurance ride, which would be coming up soon. Yes, this was place was ideal!

All too soon we returned to the barn, horses sweaty and
tired and I was once again amazed at Darrell's lack of
equine etiquette! Gently setting my saddle on the rail of
the stable door after removing it from Brumby's back,
he once again got a thorough head to toe grooming. I
watched in almost disbelief when Darrell merely pulled
his saddle and sweaty saddle blanket from Kook's back,
dumping it unceremoniously on the ground before leading
the horse out to the field where his mares awaited him.
No brushing, no hoof picking, no grooming at all! Was this
considered the cowboy way? I knew he cared for the horse;
you could tell just by the way he spoke to him. I also
couldn't help but notice how he sat so easy and relaxed
in the saddle, his hand soft on the reins, his baseball cap
tipped back at a rakish angle. He was a skilled and natural
rider, but in the stable management department, there was
obviously room for improvement!

Making sure Brumby was well settled in his paddock and politely saying my goodbyes, my saddle, bridle and grooming box were stowed away in my car. As Jasper and I left the big house on Terry Drive I could not help glancing back to where Darrell stood watching me drive down the lane. Heading back to the little trailer on the Bar-Shoe, I found my mind drifting to the quiet, dark-haired man I had just met. Somehow, he looked sad and lonely... just like me.

Chapter 15

Little did I realize it, but my life was soon to change. For the next few weeks my days were filled with driving between Bend and Redmond to my clients' farms, giving lessons and riding fractious horses. Late afternoons would see me eagerly heading towards Darrell's farm where I would spend an hour or more riding Brumby on the BLM land behind his house. As I drove down the long driveway, I could feel my heart start to race, my palms gripping the wheel that much tighter. What on earth was wrong with me? I felt butterflies in my belly reminiscent of that moment when you are in the starting box about to head out with your horse on the cross-country phase of an eventing competition! Why did my eyes immediately look towards the big house, hoping to see Darrell's work truck parked by the garage? Sometimes it would be there; more often however it was not. Obviously, he was still at work, tending to the affairs of Darrell's Electric, the electrical contracting business he owned.

Through Herb, gossipy old chap that he was, I came to discover Darrell was not married to Sonja after all. They had been divorced for nigh on ten years but still owned the house and farm in partnership together – a rather odd situation I thought! Apparently, the reason she spent so much time at the big house was due to it being up for sale. Darrell had built the house for Sonja years ago, but as their marriage started to unravel, it was sold to some ex-baseball player who ultimately defaulted on the loan. The farm subsequently reverted to Darrell and Sonja, who by that time, were divorced but still liable for the hefty loan payments.

So maybe that was why Darrell always looked so sad and lonely. He looked as if he did not belong in such a humongous house. Not that he didn't look distinguished, he just looked as if he would be more at home leaning on the doorframe of a warm, cozy cabin rather than a mansion. Now where on earth did a thought like that come from, I wondered? Here I was, in the process of going through divorce proceedings with George and, over the past year, had decided horses were considerably preferable companions to men! Yet somehow, I was drawn to this man Darrell, even though we hardly ever spoke.

I cannot deny in some ways I felt distressed my marriage to George was soon to be officially over. Why might one ask? Well, it made me feel like a failure. Despite not being happy, inside I still held to the thought that I had taken, at least what I believed to be, sacred vows of marriage. Nevertheless, there was a part of me, a growing part of me, that was starting to say, "You are an independent woman! Look at you! Making a life for yourself, managing on your own, making enough money to live. Okay, so maybe you are not rich, but you're happy, aren't you?"

Yes, that little voice would comfort me. Funny, once I make up my mind to do something, I go forward towards that goal with all my heart and soul. George told me to hire a lawyer and begin the divorce proceedings, saying it would be of benefit to me if I were "The Petitioner" as he phrased it. Of course, I did as I was told. The gentleman who represented me, as I came to discover much later on, did not exactly act in my best interests. However, once I came to terms with the fact that George and I would never reconcile, all I wanted was for everything to be over and done with. I agreed to anything at all that was proposed without question. I just wanted to be able to get on with my life, to move forward.

In no time at all, George's lawyer had a multitude of paperwork ready for me to sign. I was expected to relinquish all rights to any interest In Computer Specialist's Northwest and Whittington, Incorporated. This latter enterprise was a company of some kind George had set up just before we went our separate ways. The name Whittington was actually my idea. He was looking for a unique title for the company, one that gave connotations of wealth. The story of Dick Whittington, a poor English lad in the late 1300s who made his way to London expecting to find the streets paved with gold, came to my mind. I related the tale to George, complete with the storybook ending of when Dick Whittington ultimately became Lord Mayor of London. Anyway, since I had always thought I had nothing to do with these companies, it did not concern me at all to sign away any claim on the dotted line.

While the divorce proceedings slowly ground forward, I kept myself busy. The first endurance ride Brumby and I competed in was held east of Bend, at Horse Ridge. We were entered in the 25-mile race, the lowest mileage class but a good place to start out. The other competitors were so friendly and helpful, making me, a neophyte in this sport, feel right at home! Brumby was a trooper! He was raring to go as we watched the 100-mile competitors, mainly mounted on fit and trim Arabians, heading out on the trail in the early dawn light. Then it was finally our turn. Of all the competitions I have competed in, from jumping to dressage, being out on the trails of an endurance ride was surprisingly thrilling to me! Sometimes we would see other horses and riders ahead of us; sometimes there was just my spotty Brumby horse and I following the well-marked trail. Brumby had a most wonderful long trot and seemed to eat up the miles between checkpoints. This, our first competition, saw us coming in third in our class, winning me a cooler and praise from many of the seasoned riders. I felt elated and so proud of my little spotty Brumby horse!

I was hooked! Thankfully, Herb was a willing to chauffeur, hauling us from one ride to another. I could tell Brumby would never be a 100 miler, but I was happy competing in 25- and 30-mile races for now. Our next event was to be the Paulina Peak Ride in which I was entered in the 30-mile class. It was to be held on the Fourth of July and would be the most challenging competition for us so far. The terrain was steep and rocky, a much more grueling ride than at Horse Ridge, but I felt we were up to it.

One day, coming back to the barn after riding Brumby on the BLM trails, Darrell came strolling over to the barn.

"I hear you're going to have a competition on the fourth," he said, leaning up against the stable door, watching while I brushed Brumby down.

"Yes, a 30-mile ride at Paulina Peak," I replied, feeling my face blush.

"If I drove down there, would you come to the rodeo with me?"

"Yes," I heard myself reply, looking up at him with a smile. "Yes, I would like that very much. I've never been to a rodeo before." So just like that Darrell asked me out on a date. Well, I considered it a date!

The Fourth of July finally arrived, and the ride was all I could have hoped for, challenging, exhilarating and all too soon over. Once again, Brumby and I came in a very respectable third but more thrilling was winning the "Best Conditioned Novice Horse" award! That to me was priceless! I had just finished getting Brumby cooled down, groomed, watered and with a nice meal of hay in front of him when Darrell drove up. Herb planned on hauling Brumby back to Bend and would take care of getting him settled in his paddock for me. Darrell arrived driving his black, 1961 Chevy Impala convertible. As I climbed in beside him, feeling more than a little self-conscious, we headed down the dusty road towards my first ever rodeo adventure.

The Paulina rodeo at that time was a small affair. The kind of rodeo such as small towns all over the country used to have. Nothing fancy, just a place and opportunity for local ranching folk to get together for a good time. Sitting on the wooden bleachers beside Darrell, plastic cup of beer in hand, we watched wild horse races, wild cow milking – now that was a fun affair! – as well as the usual bucking bronco, calf roping and bull riding events. Darrell's sister Ruth and a friend of hers arrived, joining us on the bleachers. What a lovely lady! She made me feel so at ease and welcome. The rodeo was soon over for the day and as Darrell drove us back to the farm in Bend, the conversation was easy between us. After a quick check on Brumby, I loaded a very excited Jasper into Morris and set off down the driveway. In the rearview mirror I could see Darrell watching, then saw his hand raise in a wave. My heart leapt and a grin came unbidden to my face. Was this, I wondered, to be an omen of things to come?

Our next outing was to the Prineville horse races a little later in the month. We laughed and joked as we picked our favourite steeds, watching as they sped around the track. Darrell was so easy to be around, quiet, courteous, and a real gentleman. Once again driving the '61 Impala, he had picked me up at my little trailer house by the railroad track on the Bar-Shoe. Driving down the bumpy track towards the highway, he stopped at the rickety main gate. I hopped out to open it for the car to pass through before conscientiously closing it and jumping back into the red leather interior of this classic old car. It might have been a car almost as old as me, but goodness could it go! When we reached the highway, Darrell, a big grin on his face, gunned the motor and the force pinned you to your seat! It was thrilling!

After an exhilarating time at the races, night closed in, and it was finally time for me to head home as I had a busy day ahead. Dropping me off at the front door of my rickety old trailer, he leaned forward and gave me a gentle kiss goodnight. Standing on the doorstep, I waved until he was out of sight yet remained there for a while, listening. I could hear the car's big engine purring as it made its way down the track, knowing by the sound when Darrell had reached the gate. I found myself listening hard, hoping against hope that I wouldn't hear the car's engine fading away, but instead, hear it returning. It did not. Surprised at the disappointment and heaviness in my heart, I turned and went inside, closing the door firmly behind me. That night was one I shall never forget.

Chapter 16.

Surprisingly, a change had come over me. Crawling into bed in my little trailer by the railroad tracks, I felt something I had never felt before. A stirring inside that I could not name. Ginger cat curled up next to my pillow, Jasper lay heavy across my legs, a comforting weight as I tried to go to sleep. Sleep would not come.

As I tried to quiet my mind, I realized Darrell kept popping into it! Why was I thinking of him? I had no aspirations of ever getting married again, did not want a man in my life; in fact, I had resolved to stay on my own forever and focus on building up my little horse business. So why was I finding myself drawn to this quiet, charming man?

The next few days saw me diligently sticking to my schedule of visiting clients, giving lessons and riding their horses. Yet I found myself becoming anxious as the working day drew to an end, more than ready to speed off to the Terry Drive house where Brumby – and Darrell – awaited. After heading out on the BLM for an invigorating ride on my little spotty horse, sometimes, if Darrell was home from work, we would spend a few minutes chatting before I headed off home. Our conversations were polite and brief, maybe, I thought to myself, his gentle kiss goodnight was merely that of a friend to a friend and nothing more.

Frequently, one of our main topics of conversation was Darrell's stallion, Kook. This fine horse was a gentle soul, the most gentle, well-behaved stallion I had ever been around. Out in the field with his small band of mares and one of his sons – an unruly colt who would one day steal my heart – Kook was a sight to behold as he arched his neck and looked every part King of his Realm. But Kook had a problem, a growing problem, that was ominous in nature. One of his testicles was considerably larger than the other and that suggested a tumour of some kind had taken hold.

"I'm taking him to the vet tomorrow to get that looked at." Darrell said as we leaned on the fence, watching Kook grazing in the field. "He's been with me since he was six." I could tell this weighed heavy on Darrell's mind. He might not spend as much time primping and pampering Kook like I did Brumby, but I knew he had a deep love for this horse. As we stood there, the urge was strong to put my arm around him; however, I did not. Shyness held me back. After the races, we would chat when we saw each other but the kiss had not been repeated, much to my chagrin. Saying I would see him tomorrow when I came to ride Brumby, I loaded Jasper into Morris and drove away.

The following morning, dressed in my working attire of jodhpurs and riding boots, faithful Jasper sitting in the passenger seat beside me, I headed off down the Bar-Shoe's bumpy track towards the highway, turning towards Bend where my first horse of the day would be waiting for his training session. Deciding to take the back road, which was unusual for me, I made a turn at Deschutes Junction, which was a slightly longer but less travelled route to where I was going. All of a sudden, I recognized Darrell's truck and horse trailer coming towards me. He must be on his way to the vet's office in Redmond I thought. Something welled up inside me, an almost frantic desire to be with him. Not caring about road rules, I cranked the wheel around on my little beetle bug and sped after the rapidly disappearing truck and trailer. Morris seemed to nearly be up on two wheels as I careened around the corners, Jasper's claws dug into the seat to keep his balance.

Darrell finally caught sight of me in his rearview mirror,

tearing along behind him, and pulled over to the side of the road.

"What are you doing here?" he asked, jumping out of the truck. "I just saw you heading the other way towards Bend!"

"I want to come with you to the vet's office," I replied, half afraid he would say there was no need.

"But what about your work? Didn't you have lessons and stuff to do today?"

"Well, yes, but I can call them from the vet's office, they will understand. I'll tell them there is a horse emergency; after all, there is!" I followed him to the clinic at a more sedate rate and made my calls to everyone on my list for the day. Apologizing profusely for missing my appointments, they did indeed understand.

I was glad I came. Kook ended up having the testicle with the tumour – which did turn out to be cancerous – removed. Martin Warbington, Darrell's vet did not want to totally geld Kook, saying the other testicle appeared to be clean and at Kook's advanced age, to totally geld him might be awfully hard on him. Kook was going to be okay. As we stood by the pen, watching the old horse come round after the operation, I could see the relief on Darrell's face, and this time I did put my arms around him.

That day marked a turning point in our friendship. Without actually expressing how we felt in words, a feeling of warm companionship sprang up between us. Little did I know how my life would once again soon be changing and, of all things, I owed it to rats.

Yes, rats! Pack rats to be exact. Noisome, smelly, destructive creatures that are the bane of anyone living in the dry desert areas of central and eastern Oregon! Pack rats have a tendency to move in wherever they think they will find food, warmth and a nice dark place to sleep. Looking like a furry Chinchilla – I am sure they are related – pack rats do look kind of cute, that is until you come to know them a little better! Able to chew through virtually any material, squeeze through the smallest of spaces, they line their nests with anything – and I mean anything – they can pick up in their mouths. A pack rat nest can contain everything from dead birds to nails, to pieces of glass and tin and, what is worse, dried droppings from any animal. The nests can grow to tremendous proportions. They, unlike most creatures, have no problem using their nests as toilets and the waste products from pack rats' stink!

My little abode on the Bar-Shoe by the railroad tracks was the perfect haven for these rodents and was infested with them. The trailer, as I have mentioned, was an ancient, single wide dwelling, set on blocks as opposed to a true foundation. It was dark and dingy no matter how well scrubbed it might be. The electrical wiring was suspect, as I discovered one day when I climbed on the counter to reach a high cupboard and simultaneously touched the 'fridge and the stove top. The shock made me yelp and just about fall off my perch! Despite keeping all my food in cupboards and closed containers, droppings would appear overnight on my well-washed kitchen counters. The telltale smell of pack rat permeated the small back room where my meager belongings were stored in boxes, boxes that soon had holes chewed in them. What was worse were the night-time roaming, the rustling and scratching and tail thumping inside the walls by my head.

Okay, I know what you must be thinking, "Well, she has a cat! Why doesn't the cat keep the rats at bay?" I have discovered there are two types of cats in this world, rodent rustlers and bird batters. Ginger Cat obviously was of the latter variety! Although one night, all that changed. Finally becoming accustomed to the nighttime noises of what must be a huge family of rats living in the walls, I dozed off to sleep only to be rudely awakened by bedlam on the bed! As one rat scurried across my pillow, a second made a dash across the covers causing Jasper to leap to his feet. Another rat made a wild run for freedom and Jasper was on it in a flash. Ginger Cat decided to join the fray while I was yelling and thrashing about trying to bash the rat that once again zoomed across my pillow. Being blind as a bat without my glasses, my vain attempt to bash said rat failed miserably but Jasper and Ginger Cat were having better luck.

Now I am normally unconcerned about the presence of rodents, having tended many during school holidays as a child. Rats, mice, hamsters, gerbils, they hold no terror for me. However, being inundated with smelly pack rats – each weighing in the neighbourhood of a pound – chewing, gnawing and destroying everything in sight was one thing. Being part of a mass rat fight in the middle of the night, well, that was just too much! I decided it was about time to find somewhere else to live.

Later that day, feeling tired and a wee bit down in the dumps, I made my way to the Terry Drive house, almost deciding to forego riding Brumby for a day. As always of late, I was hoping Darrell would arrive home before I left. As Brumby softly nickered and came up to greet me at the paddock fence, my mind was filled with how I was going to find, and afford, a new place to live. Deciding a ride might do me good, I saddled up and headed out on the trails, content to let my little horse stroll along on a loose rein. My horse business was steadily growing but my bank account was not. The little I was making was sustaining me but the process of going through a divorce – with me as the petitioner since George told me that was what I had to be – had steadily eaten away at any savings I had accrued. Lawyers do not come cheap!

How complicated could a divorce be? I had already agreed to walk away from the house, the newer car, all the furnishings and comfortable things a home contained. I had signed over any interest I supposedly had in George's companies, which to me were just words on a bit of paper. He was making sure I left just as I came into the marriage in 1980. Less in fact, since somewhere along the lines there was that money borrowed from my father. Somehow, I did not have to sign my interest in that over to him! So technically, did this mean I still owed half of a $53,000 note? No, I would not think about it, I would put it out of my mind. The divorce papers had been signed on July 27th by both George and me. The judge added his signature on July 31st making me a free woman now -- although the divorce would not be considered legally finalized until August 31, 1987.

My optimism of always trying to look on the bright side of things occasionally fails me. The thought of trying to find a new place to live, an economical place to live, was constantly niggling in the back of my mind. There was also the challenge of having Jasper and Ginger Cat. I could never give them up even knowing many places were not open to permitting pets. Yes, I was down in the dumps. Brumby must have sensed my melancholy mood as he plodded along like an old campaigner.

As I rode slowly back to the barn, my heart lifted when I saw Darrell's work truck parked by the house. What was it with that man that my heart rate went up just with the thought of seeing him? But there he was, as I came around the corner, leaning against the barn door, waiting for me.

"Hi! How was your ride?" he asked as I jumped down

and led Brumby into the barn aisle to remove his tack and groom him.

"Good! He just loves to get out on the trails. Sometimes I wonder if he ever gets tired of wanting to see what is over the next hill although we actually just strolled along today," I replied as I vigorously brushed the little horse.

"You seem a bit quiet today. Anything wrong?" he said, a note of concern in his voice. Putting a smile on my face as I stood up after picking out Brumby's hooves, I tried to make my voice nonchalant before I replied, trying to keep the sadness at bay.

"Well, I am going to have to find a new place to live and I just don't know where to start." I could feel tears pricking at my eyes.

"Put the horse away and come tell me about it." He said, walking with me towards Brumby's paddock, opening the gate and waiting while I slipped the halter from the horse's head, watching while Brumby proceeded to have a good roll in the dust.

Walking back to the house I found myself pouring out the tale of the rats in the trailer, culminating in the melee on my bed involving a cat, a dog and what seemed like a myriad of rats. I could see Darrell trying hard to keep from grinning as I painted the picture of bedlam from the other night, but then, a sober expression crossed his face when I told him I just had to find another place to live.

"I know I should be grateful to have that little trailer, but the rats are driving me out! I just don't know where I will find a place where I can keep Jasper and Ginger Cat." There were the tears threatening to fall again.

"You could always move in here. There's more than enough room in this place and you're here every day to ride anyway." Darrell said quietly, glancing sideways at me. My heart seemed to skip a beat. He already had Herb living in the basement apartment and another friend of his staying temporarily in one of the rooms upstairs. Would there really be room for me? The house was plenty big enough.

"Do you mean it? I can't afford much in the way of rent, but I can help take care of the place and cook and clean. My business is growing, and I have a couple of customers who would like me to work with their horses on a daily basis." I could tell I was starting to babble.

"Well, there's plenty of room in the barn if you wanted to bring a horse or two here to work. The house is for sale, but it could be a while before that happens. So don't worry. Let's get you out of that trailer." His smile warmed my heart.

Within a few days I had left the Bar-Shoe behind me and was living in a light, airy room in Darrell's large house. Seldom seeing any of the other occupants of the place, it was almost like having a house of my own. I shared the kitchen with Darrell, reveling in the old, antique wood cookstove that dominated the center of the kitchen, reminding me of the Aga cookers back in England. The house truly was huge. Never one to be impressed by fancy houses, the kitchen immediately became my favourite room. Each day, I found myself looking forward to when Darrell would arrive home. His quiet companionship put me at ease. Somehow, we could talk so easily to each other, as if we had known each other for years instead of a few weeks. Such as the night when a spectacular thunderstorm lit up the sky and we found ourselves lying side by side on the floor, watching nature's fireworks through the large picture window in the dining room. We talked for hours and hours, realizing just how much we had in common. As I finally headed off to my room and he to his, he took my hand and once again gently kissed me as he had that night at the Bar-Shoe. I knew then that our relationship was about to change.

Chapter 17.

Funny, love is something you think you know, you thought you had experienced it before. Yet when love ultimately enters your life you suddenly realize those feelings you thought were love before, were nothing but a pale imitation. I was in love, truly in love, for the first time in my life. It came suddenly, like a whirlwind, with little warning. I knew I had found the man I wanted to spend the rest of my life with.

One afternoon, as I stood in the kitchen washing dishes, Darrell, just arriving home from work, walked up and put his arms around me.
"We do have a dishwasher you know," he said with a smile.
"I know," I replied, reaching for a tea towel to dry my hands. "It's just I have never used one and can't see the point really." I turned and looked up at him. Keeping one arm around my waist, he drew a ring out of his shirt pocket and without preamble, asked me to be his wife. We had only known each other for little over a month yet I knew in my heart I had found my soulmate. Without hesitation I said, "Yes!" As he wrapped me in his arms my heart overflowed. We might be seen as an unlikely couple to some, there being 24 years difference in our ages. Did it bother us? Not at all! At 26 I was an "old soul," wise beyond my years as many people had told me and Darrell at 50 was so young at heart. Thus, we fit perfectly in the middle.

My divorce papers were finally processed on August 31, officially making me a free woman and that was to be the date of our marriage. We planned on a simple ceremony right here at the house with only Darrell's children and few friends present. Nothing fancy, nothing elaborate, for this was to be our special day.

Over the past couple of months, a reconciliation of sorts
had happened between my father and me. He had reached
out and so I had tentatively renewed my relationship with
him. He was still living in Burnaby, British Columbia, but
drove his little motorhome down to Arizona on a regular
basis to join up with some of his square-dancing pals. The
first few meetings with him were tense – at least on my
part – as my conscience troubled me. For even though it
was George who absconded with my father's money, I still
felt responsible, felt I had a debt owing I could never fully
repay. Shrugging off my apologies and worries, my father
assured me he just wanted to be part of my life again.
"Really?" I thought. That didn't sound like Tom Forster,
the person to whom every penny counted! But I would
take him at his word, although knew he would always find
a way to never let me forget. On one of his visits as he
passed through Bend on his way to Arizona, over a cup of
tea he told me about finding where George and I lived after we left Vancouver – although not in what way! Relating
how he discovered where I worked and even followed me
home one wintry night to Sally's little house near Sisters,
confirming it was indeed him who had roused Jasper that
cold, black night. He even knew about my divorce. Oh yes,
a canny detective was my father!

In some ways I was glad to have my father was back in my
life. In other ways, I must admit, I was not. He was incredibly hard to please. When I wrote and told him about Darrell, he seemed happy for me. A little concerned about the
age difference between us – a bit rich coming from him,
considering he had married a woman much younger than
himself! – but his stock comment was he just wanted to see
me happy. Finally, Darrell and my father met. Both were
cordial and seemed to get along, although I could tell Darrell immediately saw my father had a definite controlling
side to him!

Shortly after returning home to Canada, my father was soon readying himself for another jaunt down to Mesa, Arizona, his favourite square-dancing destination. Writing to tell me he might pop in on his way by, he neglected to say when exactly it would be. Knowing my father, it could be within a couple of days or a fortnight away! As it turned out, it was only a few days later and in the middle of the night! The one and only time he did such a thing I might add. For on that inauspicious night, the sound of someone stealthily entering the kitchen downstairs abruptly woke us from a sound sleep. Darrell jumped out of bed and grabbed the gun that always lay to hand on the bedside table. Quietly he made his way to the landing overlooking the kitchen area below. Calling out, "Hold it right there!" in a commanding voice, he flipped the light switch on the wall beside him and the kitchen below was suddenly flooded with light, stopping the intruder in his tracks. Imagine the shock on my father's face as he looked up and saw Darrell on the balcony, gun in hand, ready to roust the suspected burglar! My father learned a lesson that night, that Darrell was one person who would stand up and fight for what was his. Too bad he didn't remember that.

As our wedding day drew near, history seemed to be repeating itself. As had happened before, my father's attitude took a turn for the worst. His letters to me became briefer, and bitterness and sarcasm were lacing his words. Reluctantly declaring he would still come to the wedding, inside me I knew he would not. Somehow, he had an uncanny way of casting a pall over what should be my brightest of days. Yet I had changed, I was not quite the same young girl I was who had married George years ago. I was a different person now and found I could withstand, to a degree, the discord my father was trying to spread. There was someone standing strong beside me now, someone who loved me dearly and accepted me just the way I was. Darrell did not want to transform me or mold me into something different; he just wanted me to be me.

I was still driving my little Morris car back and forth each day as I made my rounds to my clients' farms for lessons and horse training sessions. Darrell had tried to get me to use one of his pick-up trucks as my day-to-day vehicle as his opinion of Volkswagens was somewhat negative! As he said, there had been too many times when driving to work he had made use of his fire extinguisher to help put out engine fires in Volkswagens! When it was discovered Morris had a fuel leak, that was it. Darrell put his foot down and I found myself driving his little yellow pick-up truck with a lumber rack on top and "Darrell's Electric" emblazoned on the sides. Actually, this turned out to be very good move as I was to discover just a few days later.

The Terry Drive house was situated at the end of a long driveway with a fancy white fence bordering the two large fields that lay on either side of the lane. In the green field to the left as you approached the house and barn, Darrell's horses grazed along with three young Herefords, two steers and a heifer. Over the years, Darrell had owned numerous cattle but the downturn in the economy and financial crisis of the mid 1980s had forced him to sell all his livestock and many other assets just to keep his head above water. Right before we met, always a rancher at heart, he had bought the three yearlings, deciding to once again rebuild his cowherd.

The economic downturn had not been kind to Darrell. As one of the largest electrical contractor shops in Central Oregon, Darrell was hit hard. For a while it seemed as if the sky was the limit in the building trade, business was great! New houses and commercial buildings were springing up everywhere and Darrell, like many other contractors, felt there was no end in sight to these booming times. Then, the bottom dropped out from under everyone. Building contractors fled Bend in the middle of the night – literally – leaving buildings unfinished and bills unpaid. Many sub-contractors declared bankruptcy to avoid paying the outstanding material bills racked up on jobs no one would finish. Darrell could also have taken this easy way out but instead chose to work his way out of debt. Cutting his staff down to himself and one employee, Darrell battled on. Being unable to make payments on his farm in Culver, where he lived at that time, he had no choice but to let the bank take it back. Selling off cars, farm equipment and livestock, he struggled to make ends meet.

It was around this same time he and Sonja had to take back the Terry Drive house. Darrell built the house back in the late '70s for Sonja. She wanted a grand house that befit the lifestyle of someone married to one of the leading contractors in Bend. Divorcing shortly after the house was completed, they retained partnership in the property when it sold to the retired baseball player who subsequently reneged on the mortgage loan when times got tough. This was why the house was for sale and why Darrell was living there when I met him. Darrell never really liked the huge house but loved the land. The baseball player had made few improvements on the place other than having the driveway lined with what was then considered a novel type of fencing – wooden planking encased in white vinyl. A nice-looking fence, imitating the classic white painted board fencing popular at that time, but not the best of designs! The fence posts were lodged in the ground with concrete but the plank's vinyl covering did not seal the wood, so water and moisture could seep in. This made the wooden boards inside the vinyl prone to rotting after a few years, something I was to be very thankful for!

Our wedding day was fast approaching. To say I was feeling nervous would be an understatement! I had no doubts about Darrell and me, of that I was certain. What worried me was his family. When Darrell asked me to marry him, I accepted without hesitation as the feelings I had for this man were beyond description. I knew and accepted the age difference between us, knew he had three children from his previous marriage to Sonja and knew they were somewhat close to my age. How close I did not exactly know or care. It wasn't important to me and not something we ever discussed. Darrell's son, Andy, lived in Bend and worked side by side with his dad as an electrician. Andy was only six years younger than me – the same age as my stepsister Sarah – and we got along famously! So surely it would be the same with Darrell's other children, two daughters, Terresa and Susan. They were both married and lived in Portland on the west side of Oregon. Just days before the wedding, I met Darrell's girls at his shop in Bend for the first time and that is when it hit me how close we were in age. Although polite and courteous to me, I will admit, it was a somewhat tense meeting. Terresa, Darrell's oldest daughter, was only one month older than me and Susan, Darrell's middle daughter, had a babe in arms – I was to enter this family as a grandmother!

It must have been an equal surprise for them as it was for me! Here I was, the same age as them, marrying their father. Did they, like many of Darrell's friends, feel I was just another "gold digger"? Someone marrying their dad not for love, but for what he supposedly had, here one minute and gone the next? Suddenly, as we stood there, awkwardly trying to make conversation, I asked myself what on earth I was doing? Would I ever be able to convince them I was deeply in love with this man? I could see the reservation – or was it resentment? – in their eyes as they met me. The last thing I wanted was to come between Darrell and his children. Despite their mother and father being divorced for nearly 10 years, I felt like an interloper.

These thoughts and others like them, haunted me. So, it was no surprise they were tumbling around in my mind as I drove home on autopilot down the long driveway after a long day of riding. Glancing to my left, instinctively looking for the horses in the field, I caught sight of one of the Hereford steers lying flat on his side, legs extended straight out and head back. Waking up from my reverie, my eyes glued to his still form I thought, "He's dead!" Right about that time the truck hit the fence.

Now the driveway, as I have mentioned before, was long and straight and smooth. After being gone all day, I always tended to drive a wee bit faster than I should down the lane, thus, when I hit the fence, I really hit the fence! Before I thought about taking my foot off the accelerator, I had wiped out a good portion of the posts and rails on the right-hand side of the driveway. Planks flew high in the air. Thankfully, the steel lumber rack on the truck prevented a post, complete with huge chunk of concrete attached, from coming entirely through the windshield into the cab. The front fender and side of the little truck took a royal beating! At the noise, the supposedly dead steer, raised his head to see what all the commotion was about.

Pulling into the driveway in front of the garage, I shakily got out to survey the damage. There was a lot of damage! Making my way into the house and rushing upstairs to the bedroom, the tears began to flow. What on earth would Darrell say when he got home? Fear and anxiety filled me. My mind went back to my father, to George, knowing what they would have said, what they would have done, how they would have reacted to the accident. Before I knew it, I heard Darrell come rushing into the kitchen below.

"Rose! Where are you?" There was panic in his voice, not anger. I sat on the edge of the bed, staring out the window, tears running down my face as he bounded up the stairs and came into the bedroom. Taking me in his arms, I sobbed even harder. "Talk to me! What's wrong? Tell me what's wrong!" he pleaded.

Through my tears I could not believe he wanted to know what was wrong! Surely he saw the fence; surely he could not have missed the damage to the truck? How could he be asking me what was wrong!

"Didn't you see the truck?" I managed to say between sobs. "Aren't you angry with me?"

"Angry with you? Of course not! How could I be angry with you? What's wrong?" As he held me tight to him, I blurted out the story of seeing the steer in the field, thinking he was dead, then hitting the fence and being so afraid of what he would say when he got home.

"Oh, my dear, I don't care about the truck! When I came in and found you here crying, I thought you had decided you didn't want to marry me! I wouldn't blame you, I'm an old man and you're so young. You can change your mind you know. I will understand." This brought on another round of weeping. How could I be so lucky as to find a man like this? A man who loved me unconditionally, loved me as deeply as I loved him.

My friend Kim was right. I will never forget the day I called her to share the good news, that I had found someone special, and we were to be married. Excitedly, she wanted to know all about this special man Darrell. When I got around to mentioning his age, her initial expletive was followed by a moment of silence. Her next words have remained in my heart ever since, she said, "Well, if you only have five years together and those five years are filled with happiness and love, they will be years to cherish forever."

August 31, 1987 was at last here. The wedding cake was finished, the pastries and sandwiches, cheeses, meats and various drinks were laid out and waiting. Friends were arriving, Darrell's family was downstairs and the judge who was to officiate the ceremony was ready. The day had come. Jeanne, an older lady and good friend, had leant me a lovely, long ivory-coloured silk dress to wear. Since my father, once again abstaining at the last minute from attending my marriage, Jeanne's husband Chuck stepped up as surrogate father of the bride to give me away. As I made my way down the stairs, Darrell looked up, a smile lighting his face as he awaited me at our makeshift altar. Our eyes met and held as we stood side by side and said our vows. Kissing tenderly for the first time as husband and wife, I knew in my heart I had truly found not only a husband, but a best friend, a lover and my soulmate for life.

Chapter 18.

I never thought I would ever get married again, yet here
I was, Mrs. Howe and proud to be known as such. Darrell's Electric was growing once again due to Darrell's hard
work. More clients were coming my way both for riding
lessons and horse training and we started making future
plans for the Terry Drive property. Dave – the other friend
of Darrell's who had been living in the big house – and
Herb had moved out of their own accord when Darrell and
I tied the knot. I tried to buy Brumby from Herb, but it was
in vain, as he kept him, choosing to give my little horse to
his new lady friend. The moment when Brumby left the
farm was bittersweet, I had come to love that little fellow.

Brumby took a piece of my heart with him but another
horse, Luke, more than healed the hurt. Luke was the
precocious son of Darrell's stallion and riding horse,
Cucaracha, or Kook as he was more commonly known.
Apparently when Kook was born, a cockroach had crawled
across the shoe of the owner's wife, thereby his rather
ignominious naming! Luke was coming four years old. A
beautiful golden Dun with the classic black stripe down
his back, transverse stripe across his withers, black mane
and tail and black legs from his knees down; a grand fellow
but alas not quite the temperament as a youngster as his
sire! Darrell bred and raised Luke then sold him as a green
broke colt to a friend of his who was now boarding the
young horse at the Terry Drive farm.

Luke was not a mean horse; he just had a rather playful
side that could be quite alarming. My first up close and
personal encounter with him was when I was out changing pipe in the large 30-acre field where the horses and
Herefords grazed. I had taken up this chore of a morning
so Darrell could head off to work early. On this particular

morning, I was going to move the big wheel line that was irrigating the field and was working at the main motor unit when here comes Luke, ears pinned back, barreling towards me before stopping and rearing up with a rather disturbing demeanor. I happened to have a hammer in my hand at the time and without a thought I threw it, bonking him right between the eyes while yelling "No!" in a gruff voice. That, as they say, was the beginning of a beautiful friendship.

Darrell's friend would occasionally come out, saddle up Luke and head out for a ride. I could see the fellow was not exactly a horseman and showed all signs of being rather afraid of the fractious young horse. So, to bolster his courage, a nip or two from a whiskey bottle appeared to give him the bravado to mount up! After one such ride, Luke was unceremoniously turned out into the field with much cussing on the part of his owner. Appalled to see the bloody gouge marks from spurs on Luke's sides, my blood boiled! Let it just be said, Darrell subsequently bought Luke back from the chap and presented him to me as a wedding present. For the first time in my life, after all the years of riding and competing on other people's horses, I now owned my very first horse. One that was mine, one that could never be sold out from under me. What a fine wedding gift he was and what grand pals we became. Luke held a special place in my heart and was my faithful riding companion until the day he passed away at the fine old age of 35.

Terry Drive was perfectly set up for running a horse business. The pastures and paddocks were well fenced; there was even an outdoor riding arena. The barn was spacious and inviting and acres and acres of public land adjoined the farm. The house, although grand looking, was far too large and not at all what Darrell and I would choose to live in, both preferring something less ostentatious. However, it was there, so we of course made it our home. We could make a good life here, but there would be challenges. Although we might live on beautiful acreage in a big, fancy house, we were not well off by any means; far from it! Darrell, working hard to rebuild his business, was trying to set aside money for the soon to be upcoming annual mortgage payment. On top of this, a myriad of debt – accrued during the horrendous financial collapse in the building trade in the early 1980s – hung over his head. Instead of going the easy route and filing bankruptcy, as so many of his contemporaries did, Darrell was determined to pay off every cent owing. Sonja however, still a partner on the Terry Drive farm, was eager to sell.

Apart from my equestrian business, I decided to versify, to start putting the farm to good use. Raising rabbits for food, I developed a small clientele of people eager to buy my freshly butchered bunnies. Picking up a couple of day-old Holstein bull calves, I raised them as bottle babies with the intent of eventually selling them for beef which would give us funds to buy more Hereford cattle. Chickens were soon added to supply us with fresh eggs as well as a couple of turkeys for Thanksgiving and Christmas dinner! Each morning, Darrell headed off to Bend while I took care of the farm and animals plus worked the boarded horses I had in for training. In the evenings, as we sat in the kitchen eating dinner, plans were made to improve the farm. Working up a part of the land that had been neglected for years, turning it once again into the productive hay field it once was, starting a big vegetable garden next year; yes, we had big plans. We could do it, we could make a go of things here.

Those first few months of our marriage passed quickly. It took a bit of adjusting on both our parts as we had much to contend with. Many of Darrell's friends had been very surprised when we married after such a short time knowing each other. You could see on their faces exactly what they were thinking, "First date on July 4 and married August 31? Really? Quite the whirlwind affair and she is rather young don't you think?" A common reaction, one which made me feel quite out of place especially when meeting them for the first time. Some were very polite; others however were not, often looking at me like I was a piece of meat hanging in a butcher shop window! Being a somewhat insecure young woman, I took their coolness towards me to heart.

A number of Darrell's so-called friends made the first few months of our marriage quite a trial. It was hard to come to terms with their censorship as my insecurities left me feeling inadequate and unworthy of Darrell's love. When we were together, just the two of us, I was so very happy. Then, meeting up with anyone Darrell had known for years, I found myself becoming the prickly person I was in my school days, brusque and abrupt. Darrell would tell me he knew right away when I did not like someone, and they sure knew it too! However, Darrell pointed out our life revolved around each other, not them. He made it plain to me, "You are my one and only, my wife and the love of my life!" How, I wondered, did I ever come to deserve this man?

Bill and Mina Clough, long time close friends of Darrell's, owned a mini storage business in town, which also housed their architectural service, Clough Design. Drawing house and commercial building plans for many of Bend's building contractors, their office was a favourite meeting spot for folk to gather for a drink when the workday was done. Darrell had been a regular visitor to the Clough's office before we were married and still occasionally popped in.

I would join him if I came to town, sipping on a coke pop instead of a beer or whiskey as the others did. I really liked Bill and Mina; they were always kind to me. However, a few of the contactors who routinely were there were not as welcoming. I am sure some of them tried to be nice to me, to see me as someone permanent in Darrell's life. There were many, however, who made me feel very uncomfortable and did not seem to mind showing it! I felt badly for Darrell. I never wanted to put him in the position of having to choose between his friends or me. So, at first, I tried to keep a positive attitude, to hide my hurt feelings, but he could see right through my charade.

Darrell had been in the building trade in Bend since the late 1970s. Many of the chaps who frequented the Clough's office of a late afternoon were people he had known for years from working with on building projects. Problem was, they also had known Darrell back when he and Sonja were married, and this often was brought up in conversations in my presence. In the company of some of these people, I plastered a smile on my face when they brought up the past. I tried to ignore my inner feelings when they went on about how wonderful Sonja was, so kind and caring, such a great person! Darrell would reach out and take my hand and soon find an excuse to leave. As tears threatened to leak from my eyes, he would hold me tight, telling me yet again that those who spoke so highly of Sonja had not had to live with her; they didn't really know her. Yet, in my mind she assumed the image of Wonder Woman, everyone loved Sonja! It did not matter that she and Darrell had been divorced for nearly ten years, a lot of those gathered in that office still thought of them as a couple. I was an interloper in their eyes, a moneygrubber who surely would not be around for long! They thought I was just a passing fad.

Sonja was often on my mind during those first few months of our marriage. How could she not be? She lived in Bend. Occasionally she would call Darrell if she had an electrical problem in her house – such as a bad light fixture – and of course, was still partners with him along with the Cloughs in various building projects in town. Before Darrell and I were married, Sonja invited me to lunch. Surprised she would do such a thing and curious as to what she may want, I accepted. Not much was eaten by either of us during the meeting. It was more of a dialogue on her part to let me know what she thought I was, in her words, "getting into" by marrying Darrell. He had a temper, he was stubborn, was a philanderer and actually had left her for another woman, although that had not lasted long. He drank too much and was mean. The list went on and on and on. Listening to her, all I could think of was this was not at all the man I knew and loved! Why would she be telling me all these things? After all, they had been divorced for nearly ten years!

After leaving what had been a rather tense and uncomfortable meeting, it dawned on me; she was trying to warn me away from the man she still felt was hers. Was that why she had encouraged her girls to suggest to Darrell he needed a prenuptial agreement before we got married? Darrell told me about being encouraged to have such an agreement, but we just laughed it away; it was ludicrous! At the time, I just knew Sonja had to be behind it. Her vain attempt failed, nothing was going to make me walk away from the man I loved with all my heart and whom I knew loved me just as deeply.

Did all this negativity towards me change the way I felt about my dearest Darrell? Indeed it did not. For what we had between us transcended all. We had plans; a life mapped out before us. Now if we only owned the Terry

Drive farm outright, we could get on with building our future together. After much discussion, trying to figure out how we could afford it, Darrell approached Sonja with an offer to buy her out. We really felt we could make a good life here. However, it was not to be. For whatever reason, Sonja refused to sell her share of the farm to us. Why we will never know, as a buyer soon came along and, despite the rather low offer made, Sonja insisted the place be sold. Our Terry Drive dreams dissolved; but looking back, it was very much for the best. The house, although grand, was not the sort of house Darrell nor I wanted. No worries, we thought, this would be a chance to start fresh, break all ties to the past, we would build a home somewhere just for us.

Although on the outside it may have appeared as if Darrell was quite well off, what with his old Chevy cars and his electrical contracting business, et cetera. Still in partnership with Sonja and the Cloughs on a couple of pieces of property in Bend, Darrell desperately wanted out, to sell his shares and be done with them. The reality was he was deeply in debt yet determined to pay off the accrued bills from the collapse of the real estate market a few years back. He also owned, in conjunction with fellow contractor Del Kennel, a piece of bare land east of Bend on K-Barr Road. Realizing we had to get cracking and move everything off the Terry Drive farm as soon as possible, Darrell approached Del and they worked out a deal for us to buy him out, thus owning the K-Barr land outright.

The property was very secluded, accessed by a rough county road that passed through public BLM land. A large irrigation canal split the property although the ground on the far side of the waterway was negligible. There was nothing on the land, no buildings, corrals, nothing. A couple of the open areas amongst the many Juniper trees had been turned into pasture and hay fields by Del years ago, a place for him to graze his cows. The perimeter fence badly needed repair and, other than an irrigation pond, it truly was bare land. As we stood by the edge of the pond, Darrell turned to me, "Do you think you could live out here?" he asked. "We will have to build everything from scratch, living in the camper while we do it. It'll be rough for a while, no running water, nothing. What do you think?"

"Yes!" I said without hesitation, hugging him around his waist. "Yes! We can do this."

Soon, portable corrals were set up for the horses, Darrell's old cars parked here and there under Juniper trees. His 8-foot camper was set up on blocks, our new home while we built something more permanent to live in. The animals were moved over from Terry Drive and housed in temporary paddocks set up here and there, strands of electric fence wire keeping everyone contained until new, permanent fences could be built. While Darrell headed off to work of a morning, I irrigated fields, worked on repairing the old perimeter fences and found myself constantly busy. This was going to be a lot of work, but I was in my element. After much deliberation and discussion, I decided to cut back on my teaching and horse training as more and more of my time was taken up working on our K-Barr farm.

Winter was fast approaching and, as romantic as it was living in a little camper, the thought of taking baths in the irrigation pond during the coldest part of the year was not very appealing!

"How about we build a shop and put an apartment in one end of it?" Darrell asked one day. "We could divide the building into three sections, an open-ended shop, an enclosed part to work on cars and such, then about a 1,000-square-foot apartment at the end? It wouldn't take long to build; we could be in it by winter."

"I like that idea! When shall we start?" I asked. It

sounded cozy. After all, if we could live comfortably in an 8-foot camper, a 1,000-square-foot apartment would be heavenly!

Before long, with the help of a couple of Darrell's young contractor friends, the building was up and roughed in. The apartment in the end was going to be perfect for us. A large open living area comprising of living room, kitchen and dining area with one bedroom and one bathroom, it was all we needed. From the outside, you would never know a cozy home resided in what looked like a large workshop! We were ready to move in just as winter made his appearance at the tail end of 1988. The apartment still had a way to go to be considered completely finished, but it seemed so spacious after the confines of the little camper. A lot had been accomplished in the first year of our marriage.

Just after we officially moved into our new abode, I came down with a severe case of appendicitis. Darrell rushed me to the local hospital where I underwent an emergency appendectomy. Upon my discharge, Darrell brought me home to a cold home, for there wasn't any heat installed yet. My dearest man scrambled to get something set up while keeping me bundled under the covers in bed. Getting a woodstove hooked up was the priority and soon I was recovering in front of a roaring fire.

Bit by bit our apartment was finished. Yes, it was a wee bit unorthodox as we had a wood heating stove and wood cook stove in the main living area while our electric cooker sat in the bathroom. In the next area of the shop, Darrell insulated the ceiling and walls then sectioned off a special portion, which soon became a meat cutting area complete with sink. This in turn was again partitioned off by making two additional rooms, one housing his reloading and gun smithing equipment, and the other becoming a good-sized pantry. The last section of the building was a general storage area with plenty of room to park another of Darrell's old cars.

To a lot of people, it probably was not much. It certainly was no Terry Drive mansion! From the outside it just looked like a large, brown metal-sided shop sitting amongst Juniper trees on the edge of a pasture. To us, however, it was home. Maybe there was a good reason we didn't end up with the Terry Drive farm. Maybe Fate knew what was best for us after all. The Terry Drive land was lovely as were the outbuildings, but the big house itself would always be a reminder that Sonja had lived there, that it once was her house. Our little place on K-Barr was just that... our home. Something we were building together. Something we could call our own and be proud of, something for just the two of us.

As Darrell's birthday on the last day of the year approached, we were finally settled in our new little home. There was still much work to be done but we celebrated with joy the coming of the New Year and looked forward to all 1989 had in store for us.

Chapter 19.

1989. A year that would see a major change of direction
in our lives, a year that brought us even closer than ever
together. We celebrated the New Year happily ensconced in
our little apartment in the end of our shop on the K-Barr
land. Slowly, slowly over the next few months our farm
grew in leaps and bounds. Added to the modest but growing herd of cows and hens were meat chickens, turkeys,
more rabbits and pigs.

While Darrell was at work wiring houses, I ran our farm.
Irrigating the fields, fixing fences, tending the livestock and
building up our new endeavour kept me busy. From humble beginnings on Terry Drive, our little meat business was
growing! After raising up the little dairy calves to full grown
steers, they were eventually dispatched and sold as beef to
some of our friends. The proceeds from this venture went
into buying bred beef cows to expand our herd. When
some of our customers learned I was raising rabbits for
meat, a new business opportunity presented itself. Soon
the rabbit herd expanded to where I was dispatching eight
to ten rabbits every second Tuesday and made deliveries to
my customers around Bend the following day. From rabbits, the requests started coming in for chicken. Why not,
I thought! So fifty Cornish Cross meat chicks were bought
and soon fresh chicken was added to our provisions list.
If we were raising chickens, why not add in a few Thanksgiving and Christmas turkeys too? Yes, our farm and little
meat business as well as Darrell's Electric was thriving!

One of my daily delights was to meet Darrell wherever
he was working so we could have lunch together. It was
impractical for him to dash home at noon each day since
we lived on the outskirts of town and usually miles from
the jobsite. Instead, I would make a proper dinner, load

it all up in the truck and drive to wherever he was so we could have our mid-day meal together. Now this was not just sandwiches and snacks. No indeed! It was a full course meal consisting of meat, mashed potatoes, vegetables, gravy and even dessert, complete with crockery and cutlery. The other chaps on the jobsite would look on in wonder as we ate our hot meal while they pulled sandwiches out of their bait boxes! This truly was the highlight of my day.

Thankfully, Darrell was a good old meat and potatoes man. He was willing to try anything… once… and for the most part ate up what I cooked with relish! However, his first encounter with a steak and kidney pie, although he ate it up, proved to not be one of his favourite dishes. Now the raccoon pie… that was another story!

As I have mentioned before, Darrell loved old Chevy cars! From his very smart 1961 Impala SS convertible to the old 1955 Bel Air convertible in parts and pieces – most would refer to it as a "basket case" – he had a few others in various stages of repair. What fun it was to be out in the shop with him while he rebuilt an engine or rewired one of the old cars. Before long, I was hooked and became owner of a 1967 El Camino in need of a lot of restoration. However, I am getting ahead of myself! You are no doubt still wondering about the raccoon pie, which, believe it or not, totally ties in with old cars.

Now when one is restoring any type of classic car you need replacement parts. One can either order from a catalog or better yet, attend a swap meet where bargaining for just the right price on an old treasure is the norm rather than the exception. Darrell and I made a trip to the Willamette Valley – on the far west side of Oregon – in order to attend the Albany car swap meet. Making a fun trip out of it, we took the pick-up just in case we discovered an old engine,

transmission or other cumbersome item to haul home.
Once our browsing was done and a few odds and ends
safely secured in the bed of the truck, we began the long
journey home. I was driving, cruising along at a comfortable highway speed, when all of a sudden I exclaimed "Raccoon!," slammed on the brakes and started backing up –
thankfully there were no cars behind us! "What on earth!"
muttered Darrell as I put the truck in park and leapt from
the cab. There, lying in the road, was a big raccoon.

I was not exactly thinking of dinner when I hoisted the
dead animal into the back of the truck bed, more that I
wanted to tan the hide. Jumping back into the driver's seat
we sped away as traffic drew near. I had recently started
tanning all manner of animal hides such as rabbit, deer
and coyote and had even tried my hand at a cowhide.
This raccoon would be a lovely addition to my collection
I thought. Darrell just grinned. What a patient chap he was!

Once back home, as I heaved the big, dead raccoon out of
the truck, I realized it was very fresh and in great shape!
Obviously struck in the head, as no damage was apparent
anywhere on its body. Carefully I skinned it out, taking
special attention to keeping things such as eyelashes, nose
and lips intact on the hide. What a beauty it was! Once
deprived of its fur coat, I saw that indeed there was not a
mark on the carcass. When I suggested to Darrell that we
have roast raccoon for Sunday dinner, he did not decline
the idea, just gave me another grin and said, "Why not!"
So roast raccoon it was and my goodness what a delicious
bit of meat that was, although skinned out it looked suspi-
ciously like a cat sitting there in the roasting pan!

A raccoon of this size had a lot of meat on it; hence, the
next day for our dinner at Darrell's job site, raccoon pie
was on the menu, much to the astonishment of the rest

of the crew. It proved to be one of the tastiest meat pies I have ever made!

Buying bare land and building everything on it from scratch can be a challenge and a chore. Fences to be repaired and new ones built. Accommodations for chickens and turkeys, rabbits and horses arranged. Of course, starting from scratch means you can plan precisely what you want and where it should go. Horse paddocks at first were temporary enclosures made by hooking heavy metal panels and gates together. Darrell's old stallion, Kook, was comfy in a paddock of his own close by the shop, not too far away from his small band of mares. A barn was soon constructed with a good-sized fenced, outdoor riding arena nearby. Cows were grazed contentedly in a big field, happily munching away on lush, green, irrigated pasture.

This was living the dream for both of us! We didn't need a big, fancy house; our little apartment at the end of the shop was just perfect. Soon, a big vegetable garden was in production about a hundred yards away from the house where we grew everything from cabbages and carrots to beans, corn and potatoes. Each end of the garden plot had a frame built that was then covered in heavy, clear plastic. This made a temporary greenhouse of sorts, as the Central Oregon High Desert area weather could produce an unexpected frost any day of the year! The two makeshift greenhouses provided much needed protection for the green beans growing at one end of the garden and the corn at the other. That first year we had a bumper crop of potatoes and turnips that grew bigger than Darrell's fist! Harvest sure was a wonderful time that year!

At the far end of the garden plot, we made plans to build a pigpen. The idea being that after the growing season was over we could turn the pigs into the garden plot to clean and root it up while providing good old fertilizer for the ground. Since my meat business was growing, I figured why not raise a couple of pigs, sell one which in effect would put one in the freezer for us at little to no cost. My friend Val – who I had known since my days working at the Trakehner farm – raised pigs, so we had a good source for quality weaner piglets. That day in early May – May 5 to be exact – was a scorcher as we worked away getting the final touches completed on the pigpen. Darrell and I stopped for moment when an unusual sound caught our attention. We looked to the east where the ominous sound was coming from and that was when we noticed the huge black cloud rolling rapidly towards us.

"What on earth is that?" I asked, standing and shading my eyes from the sun as I stared at the unusual cloud.
"I don't know!" Darrell replied, dropping his tools and grabbing my hand, "but we had better get back to the shop... and fast!" The sound can only be described as if a freight train was barreling down on us. We ran across the field just as the first hailstones began to fall. Darrell had been working on his 1961 Chevrolet Impala – the lovely black SS convertible no less – and it was sitting just outside the shop, top down, battery cables disconnected. As the huge – and I mean huge – hailstones started pelting us, Darrell grabbed a sheet of plywood, which thankfully was close by, and threw it over the car's interior, trying to give it some protection. There was no time to try to re-connect the battery cables and drive the thing into the shop as the storm was upon us. Silly me, instead of running straight into the building, I ran around the side of the shop to look and make sure the horses were okay. Not the protected west side of the building by the way, but the east side, the side the storm was coming from! Some huge bonks on the head with whopper hailstones was what I received for my moment of heedlessness!

You could not even see the horses as the torrent of hailstones came down, I could only hope they had found shelter under the trees. Kook was in his paddock just across
from the shop and although standing hunch backed under
a stout Juniper tree, he was still getting hammered. Running back out into the storm Darrell and I managed to get
a halter on him, coaxing him into the end of the shop for
some protection. As the storm intensified and the hailstone
grew in size, the noise was deafening. Even standing right
next to each other, Darrell and I had to shout to be heard
over the din. Despite being a solid as a rock horse, the
noise was too much for even old Kook. Tearing the lead
rope out of my hand he took off into the storm. Wanting to
run after him, Darrell stopped me, it was just too dangerous, we would look for him when the storm subsided.

We stood with arms wrapped around each other, watching futilely as the colossal hailstones bounced high off the
bonnet and boot of the Impala. The ground was white with
the things, many the size of tennis balls. An unopened tin
of V-8 juice had been sitting on the ground near the entrance of the shop. Remarkably it was still intact although
thoroughly beaten up – we still have that tin to this day. As
fast as the storm hit, it was over. How many minutes we
stood wrapped in each other's arms I cannot say. It seemed
like forever, but I am sure it was only minutes. As the dark
cloud rolled past, the sun came out and we left the safety
of the shop to survey the damage.

The Impala was a wreck! Thankfully the plywood had
saved the interior's leather seats from damage, but the
rest of the car looked as if some maniacal monster had
taken a ballpeen hammer to its glossy black surface! Dents
covered it from one end to the other; the fancy alumi-
num trim alongside the car was destroyed. Trees had their
leaves stripped from the branches. The ground was slip-

pery with hailstones. Thankfully, the horses and cows had
found enough shelter under trees to weather out the storm
without injury, but where was Kook? Briefly we wondered
what devastation Bend had suffered, as that was where
the storm seemed to be heading. Grabbing another halter
and lead rope, we set off to catch the old stallion, sure we
would find him with the mares and Luke.

That day and night is one I shall never forget. After hours
of searching, following then losing, then finding his trail
again, there he was, standing in someone's field a good
way from home. He looked at us calmly as we walked up to
him. Poor chap, in his terrified flight away from the storm,
he had torn through numerous barbed wire fences, cutting his chest and legs, losing a lot of blood in the process.
While I stayed with him, for he was unable to walk, Darrell
went home to get the horse trailer. Soon he was back in
his paddock, I doctored his many wounds and tough old
fellow that he was, made a full recovery. That storm was
sure one to remember. It never did make it to Bend, in fact
the residents of Bend just a mere nine miles away from us
never even knew for days there had been such an event.
Cutting a swath of destruction about a quarter mile wide
by about four or five miles long, it had only affected a small
number of people. Trees denuded of their foliage and damaged vehicles and buildings marked the storm's pathway.
Hailstones that, even a day later, were still the size of golf
balls, reminded us we had witnessed a remarkable storm.
The painful lumps on my head would also attest to that!
Oh, and on a side note, the racoon hide still hangs on our
wall to this day! Yes, those were and always will be, special
and treasured memories of a rather interesting year!

Chapter 20

Life can be so challenging at times. Through thick and thin, the ups and downs, one must hold onto the belief that Fate is throwing this at you for a reason. They say what doesn't kill you makes you stronger; well, I firmly believe in that! Although, if I am honest, I must admit over the years I have occasionally thought Fate a cruel mistress, yet in the end I have come to see she truly does know best!

When Darrell and I were first married, I was coming up on my 27th birthday and he on his 51st. The twenty-four years that separated us in age were negligible in our minds for age is just a number. It is the way one feels and acts that matters. I was an old soul for my age and he a young one, so we met perfectly in the middle. Age, then and now, means nothing to us, we were meant to be together as soulmates for life. But I am digressing.

In the past few years before Darrell and I found each other, the urge to have a family of my own had never left me. How hard it was to come to terms with what I had been told after my last miscarriage in Vancouver late in 1984, that I would never be able to bear a child. Seeing a pregnant lady could bring instant tears to my eyes. The thought of holding someone's little newborn child was unbearable. The grief that filled me sometimes overwhelmed me; I longed to be a mother.

Fate, I felt, delt me a good deed when she brought Darrell into my life. Here he was, a fine strapping chap in the prime of life who already had three grown children of his own – two were married and one had a little lad of her own. I will never forget that moment when we talked of family. It was shortly before we were to be married. I was standing in the kitchen by the sink, my bare feet cool on the floor on that hot summer day, waiting anxiously for him to arrive home from work. I had decided I must tell him my secret. Would he still want to marry me if he knew I could never bear him a child? What would he say? It was a topic of conversation that had never been broached during our many discussions of what the future held for us.

My fears, however, were unfounded. Not turning away from the sink when he came into the kitchen, as I customarily would have done, he came to my side, concern etched on his face. Gently enfolding me in his arms he asked, "What's wrong Rose?" The tears welled in my eyes as I hesitantly, then with determination, revealed to him I could never bear him a child and the reason why. Turning me towards him and gently wiping away the tears that now ran freely down my face, he held me tight.
"Oh, my dear," he gently exclaimed, "I have been trying to find the right time to tell you, I can never father another child. Yet how I would love to be able to give such a gift to you! There would be nothing that would delight me more than for us to have a child!" Warmth flooded through me for I knew he was sincere. Inside, an unexpected feeling of contentment settled on me. Although knowing we could never share the happiness of raising up a child of our own, just knowing how my dearest felt brought a heartfelt joy to my soul.

Did the feeling of sadness still creep over me when I saw a mother-to-be with her arms wrapped protectively and loving around her swollen belly? Indeed, it did. For many, many years I was unable to hold the swaddled newborn a new mother would proudly hold out towards me, seeing the confusion and, yes, sometimes hurt in their eyes as I refused their offer. Why was it new mothers always expected people to want to cuddle little babies anyway? I would smile and try to soften the refusal by saying "Not today!".

Darrell and I had been married for a couple of years and during that time, although staying pretty healthy and fit, I found myself making a trip or two to the emergency room. A sudden bout with appendicitis led to an emergency appendectomy, an old injury to my knee necessitated arthroscopic surgery and the recurrence of severe abdominal pain led me to make an appointment with a lady doctor for a much neglected female checkup!

Since I had suffered for many years from acute pain at certain times of the month, I decided to make an appointment, not with our general doctor, but with a "lady doctor," a gynecologist. East Cascades Women's Clinic in Bend was recommended to me. Entering the foyer, I felt out of place. The large, airy room was full of women in various stages of pregnancy, some alone, others with doting husbands by their sides or little children playing with toys at their feet.

My turn came and I was called back to see one of the doctors with whom I had made an appointment. She was a small, petite lady who honestly looked more like a hippy yoga teacher than a doctor at first glance! Yet she had a no-nonsense approach to her and a kindness that put me instantly at ease. Because I was a new patient, she took the time to ask a thorough medical history and since her specialty was women's health, I of course told her about my previous miscarriages and the prognosis of never being able to carry a child to full term.

After my exam, she had a quizzical look on her face. Sitting down beside me she said, "Rose, I would like to get a complete set of your medical records from your previous doctor in Vancouver to review. I will need your permission to do this and the name of the hospital where you had your procedures done. Let me bring you the paperwork."

Puzzled, but not concerned, I completed the necessary form and made a follow-up appointment for my next annual exam before leaving to head home.

A fortnight later I was back at the clinic after receiving a call from the doctor. Certain that something must be wrong, Darrell took time off work to come with me although insisted on staying in the truck in the parking lot! I did not blame him for not wanting to sit in a waiting room full of expectant mothers!

On pins and needles I waited my turn to be called back to see the doctor. Forgoing flipping through the myriad of magazines on the little tables dotting the waiting room – why couldn't they have a least a National Geographic or something other than magazines on babies to look at – I tried to imagine why I was here. With slightly shaky legs I headed back to a consulting room when my name was finally called.

When the doctor entered, she had a manilla folder tucked under her arm. Sitting down opposite me, she explained how my medical records had at first been a challenge to obtain from Dr. White up in Vancouver, but she had persisted and finally received them.

"I have some interesting news for you Rose. There is nothing wrong with you. You are a very healthy 29-year-old woman who has no reproductive issues at all. You are more than able to carry a pregnancy to term should you wish." She watched me carefully as she said this. I found myself shaking, the blood seemed to have drained down to my toes.

"But that can't be! I was told I could never carry a child to term, that I would lose the child and that it would be extremely dangerous to me too!" I could feel the tears coming on.

Putting her hand on my arm, she said gently, "It is all here in your medical records, Rose. You just had some bleeding when you thought you had your first miscarriage but the physician at the E.R. was told to terminate the pregnancy."

"But Doctor White told us it was a miscarriage!" I could feel myself coming apart.

"No, it was not diagnosed as a miscarriage, Rose. Sometimes a woman can have some bleeding during the first trimester of their pregnancy, and it does not necessarily mean they are miscarrying. Many women go on to have a healthy baby."

"But the second time," I interrupted her, "I was told it was an ectopic pregnancy which is why they had to operate on me. That was when Doctor White told me I could never carry a child again. That was true, wasn't it?" I looked in her eyes, desperately wanting her to tell me that yes, that part at least was true, but I could see the answer before she said the words.

"No, Rose, it was not an ectopic pregnancy. Your doctor scheduled you for an abortion. The paperwork may have been signed by your husband. You are a healthy young woman. You can have children. What you have been told and led to believe, what has been done to you infuriates me!" She looked at me in concern. "You are a strong woman. You will be okay."

As I dried my tears and stood up to leave, I realized this doctor was truly and fiercely disturbed by what she had discovered. She gave me a hug as we left the room, and I felt she was not the sort of person who gave hugs lightly, so her embrace warmed me. As I made my way outside, I could not wait to feel Darrell's arms about me. When he saw my face, his went white in dread as he jumped out of the truck to meet me, wondering what on earth was wrong. Tears flowed as he helped me into the front seat. With his arm firmly wrapped around me, I told him the

whole story. Anger filled his face as he clasped me tightly to
him, anger at those who did this to me, George, the doctors, all of them. As we drove home, Darrell never once let
go of my hand.

Later that night, I found, to my surprise, my heart beginning to heal. Back when we were first married and Darrell
learned how much it hurt me not to be able to become a
mother, he had talked of us adopting a child. Yet I did not
want to, for if we were to have a child, I wanted to have his
child! I thought back to my dear friend Doris with whom I
worked in the little Marc Singer shop in Vancouver and to
whom I had confided about my pregnancies. There was a
similar age difference between her and her husband Walter, she the elder of the two. Doris too loved children but
never had any. That conversation came back to me now.
  "Rose, Walter and I love each other deeply. Our lives
are perfect, and I am selfish. I have never wanted anything
to come between us and as much as I know we would still
love each other even if we had a child, I would be afraid
our love would not be as deep as it with just the two of us.
So, I am content, and Walter is content."

I had thought those were odd words to say, especially as
they came shortly after my first "miscarriage" when I was
feeling the deep sadness of losing a baby. Now I finally understood what Doris meant. My love for Darrell was sometimes frightening in its intensity as was his for me. We were
one being, soulmates forever. Fate had brought us together
for a reason. As I thought of this, I felt a sense of peace
settle over me that has never left. Yes, I understood at last
what Doris meant. Did the feeling of sadness eventually
leave me when I saw a pregnant lady? Yes, it did, but not
for many, many years afterwards. Do I regret not having
children of my own? No, not really, for I am more than content in my life. Besides, I have been – and still am – blessed

to have some wonderful children be part of my life, from grandchildren to Pony Club youngsters to children of dear friends. Fate knew exactly what she was doing when she brought Darrell and me together forever.

Chapter 21.

Our life had quickly assumed a steady rhythm of peace and contentment. Darrell and I were made for each other! Were there trials and tribulation in these early years? Oh yes indeed, but the funny thing is, all of the bumps in the road were caused by other people. In fact, that has been the way all through our many years of marriage.

Shortly after we were settled on our K-Barr farm, Darrell's longtime secretary, Jean, decided it was time to retire. Darrell's business, Darrell's Electric, Inc., had slowed down considerably over the past few years due to the big recession in the 1980s. Where he once ran a shop of fifteen employees, he now had himself and a couple of other electricians – Andy, his son being one of them. Darrell decided he no longer wanted to build back up to such a big shop again, he was staying plenty busy and was content. With the smaller shop and lightening of the workload, I felt comfortable becoming the company bookkeeper. Having no prior accounting experience, it was a wee bit daunting, but Jean took me under her wing a week before she left and gave me a rudimentary course in taking care of the company books.

Winter was upon us and after the morning farm chores were taken care of, I would head into Bend to Darrell's office. While he was out working at the jobsite, I plugged away at making sense of the books. One thing I discovered was the filing system was not exactly an efficient one! Drawers filled with a miscellany of files from years and years back were intermingled with current accounts. Folders filled with Darrell's personal information were next to old and new client's records. It was a mess! As a person who likes a logical order to things, I knew I would have to go through everything in the file cabinets piece by piece.

Reorganizing and regrouping folders so they made sense to me. In the warmth of the office on a cold, windy winter's day, this task was tedious but almost enjoyable, especially when Darrell popped in for a hug and a chat.

I say "almost enjoyable" as during the cleaning out of old records, drawers and desks I found some things that I wished I had not. Going through old redundant job files I discovered Darrell had been the electrician George had called – while we still lived in Vancouver – when the renters in the little house in Tumelo had discovered an electrical issue that needed fixing. There were also old reminders that Darrell's previous wife – not Sonja, but wife number two of short duration – had also for a while tended the books. Since I was still a somewhat insecure soul, these ghosts from the past haunted me.

Sometimes Darrell would come into the office to find me in tears, a few old letters and cards spread around me as I sat on the floor going through a dusty desk drawer. Gathering me into his arms he would ask what was wrong as I tried to wipe my eyes.

"I found these old cards and letters in the back of one of the drawers" I mumbled out, holding up a collection of old birthday and Valentine's Day cards in my hand. Many of them from a certain person in his past with terms of endearments to Darrell I did not want to see.

"I have no idea how long they have been in there in those drawers." Darrell said, holding me close. "She means nothing to me. That was one of the biggest mistakes of my life."

Having such a low self-esteem did not make these words more comforting, yet deep inside me I believed him. Sonja had tried, in that meeting before Darrell and I were married, to make me believe he was a philanderer. I did not believe it then and I did not believe it now. Had I too not made blunders in my past? As I looked into his eyes, I knew he loved me and that, I told myself, was all that mattered. The past was in the past; I was just being too sensitive, too naïve.

There was one incident however, that will forever stick in my mind, rather hilarious as I look back on it now, but not so at the time! I had been sorting through all the old files and there was a huge accumulation of past bills from a good few years ago that needed weeding out and archiving. Soon the file cabinets were organized and tidy, neatly holding folders containing current accounts both receivable and payable. As bills came in, I would scrupulously go over them to make sure the charges were correct, a small idiosyncrasy of mine I have to this very day.

It was while going over a current telephone bill that I noticed a considerable number of long-distance calls from Arizona. Arizona? Why on earth would there be calls from Arizona on our telephone bill? Calling the telephone company to rectify this obvious error, I was astounded to hear that yes indeed, the calls had been made from someone in Arizona, reverse charging the expense to our business telephone number – something one could easily do back in those days. Curious, and more than a little perturbed, I went back through old telephone bills and sure enough found several such instances! A mystery to solve, I decided to trace the person to whom these calls had been made. Calling the suspicious number, let us just say, the gentleman whom I reached on the end of the line was not expecting a lady with an English accent!

Turns out Darrell's ex-wife Diana – the one of "short duration" – now lived in Arizona. She must have been having quite the affair with this gentleman I called, who was married, by the way, and did not want his wife to know about his shenanigans when he was out of town. Diana had the audacity to be charging her long-distance calls to her gentleman friend to the Darrell's Electric's telephone number! Not only that, but I then was able to deduce that the calls we had been receiving of late, calls with no one speaking on the end of the line, were also coming from Arizona. Feeling quite outraged, I went back into sleuthing mode, eventually discovering her address and telephone number. Without hesitation, a call was made making it quite clear that if this did not stop, immediately, I would personally be making a trip to Arizona and the outcome would not be pretty! The calls miraculously stopped.

Soon all the books and files were in order. A couple of times a week I would head into the office with Darrell, settling down at the desk to pay bills, send out invoices, slowly learning the art of bidding a job from a set of blueprints. Sitting in the small room with Darrell just a few feet away was pure contentment. We were a team. Slowly, slowly the business started to build up again to where Darrell wanted it. He was able to pick and choose what jobs he and his crew wanted to take on. Accounts were reconciled in a timely manner, bills paid as they came in. Darrell worked hard, very hard, for as he said, he had a purpose in life now.

Back at home on the farm we worked diligently to improve the state of the land. The irrigation system was updated, a barn and the small outdoor paddock that doubled as a riding arena was built and fenced. The horses had snug stables with large outdoor runs attached and daily turnout in the grassy fields. Old Kook, despite having been divested of one of his testicles due to cancer, still ruled the roost and before he passed away at the ripe old age of 30, sired two more colts for us. Darrell's business was growing, and we were happy. There was, however, a dark cloud on the horizon; one, which could have torn Darrell and me apart, but instead, brought us closer than ever together. That darkness was my father.

He had always had a habit of showing up unannounced on our doorstep. Although after the instance on Terry Drive, where he could so easily have been shot as an intruder, he no longer arrived in the middle of the night! It was not, however, at all unusual for us to arrive home and find his little motorhome parked in the driveway by the shop, telling us it was to be a brief visit as he was on his way south for a couple of months. Still an avid square and round dancer, he would follow some of his friends south from Vancouver, B.C. down to Mesa, Arizona, when the weather started to turn towards winter. Although not technically a "Snowbird," as these southern migrating seniors were often called, he did enjoy heading down to hot, sunny climes when the Vancouver weather turned cold and wet.

Since my marriage to Darrell and our move from Terry Drive to K-Barr, my father had actually been quite pleasant to be around. He would occasionally show up in his Minnie Winnie motorhome, park under a juniper tree and potter about the farm helping with chores now and then. His delight seemed to be feeding the chickens and checking for eggs, a chore he did numerous times a day! He had confided in us on his last trip down that his doctor had told him to quit smoking and by gosh he had! This was a huge thing to hear as almost every year on his birthday since I was a little girl, he had sworn off cigarettes. Once, he even nailed one the last ones in the packet to the wall above the fireplace to make his point – only to have him back puffing away again before the "last cigarette" had dried out, all the tobacco falling out onto the mantelpiece I might add! Yet I was noticing a funny thing, each time he went to ostensibly check the chicken house for eggs, there was a definite aroma of tobacco smoke around him when he returned empty handed.

I eventually started enjoying the occasional visits from my father. He was amiable, courteous to Darrell, helpful around the place and never stayed long. In fact, it came to the point where Darrell even suggested making a special parking spot for my father's little motorhome.

Our property on K-Barr sat alongside a large, main irrigation canal. It looked and flowed like a rushing river from April through September's irrigation season. There was even a cascading waterfall close by. From this main canal, smaller irrigation ditches supplied water to properties sometimes a mile or more away from the main channel. Our property had such a diversion ditch cutting through it, and the small chunk of land on the far side of this ditch was an area we seldom used. Darrell thought it would be the perfect spot to set up a cement pad, complete with water and power hook-up, where my father could park his motorhome and stay for an extended period of time. In fact, Darrell went so far as to suggest we could set up an actual trailer house. What this man wouldn't do for me! Yet I had my reservations about having my father living almost year-round beside us. I knew him too well. As it turned out, it was not long before Darrell got to see the other side of Tom Forster too.

Winter was soon upon us again but this year we were snug as bugs in a rug in our little apartment at the end of our shop; it was the perfect set up! With the shop divided into three segments we had our cozy apartment, a well-insulated and heated shop section where we could work on old cars in comfort, followed by the "outer" shop, as we called it, allowed another old car and other things to be stored out of the weather. The open floor plan of our apartment was just right for us. Blue and buggy pine paneling covered the walls, I had made the curtains for the windows using Darrell's antique treadle sewing machine that, with a little tweaking, was still functionable. Our eclectic assortment of furniture, mostly Darrell's accumulation over the years, fit in perfectly. A wood stove kept us toasty warm, and an old claw-foot bathtub made my evening soaks a joy. What more could a person ask for I wondered?

Chapter 22.

Life had assumed such a comfortable routine. We continued to work and improve the K-Barr land and facilities,
improving the hay and pasture fields, working hard but
having so much fun. One of our greatest enjoyments was
taking off for the weekend, with just a few essential things
thrown in the back of the truck and heading east to fish on
the John Day River.

A dear friend of mine, Donna, would obligingly come out
to tend to the horses and other animals when Darrell and
I headed off on one of our jaunts. We had been friends
since my early days in Bend when both of us worked at the
Bon Marche department shop. Occasionally accompanied
by her young daughter Heather, Donna willingly came out
to the farm to do chores and watch over the place while
Darrell and I were gone. Donna loved the horses and so
I started giving her riding lessons, much to her delight.
When a young colt was born to our mare Candy, the horse
Donna used to ride, she immediately fell in love with the
little chap! In gratitude for all the times she came and took
care of the farm while we were off gallivanting, we gave the
youngster to her, much to her joy and surprise.

It was such fun to plan a fishing trip on the John Day. The
day before leaving on such a venture, we would either
throw a few odds and ends in the back of one of the work
trucks or have the camper loaded on the big truck so we
could sleep and camp in comfort. Heading east on the
weekends became a regular occurrence, something we
both looked forward to. It was as if the eastern side of the
state was calling to us, drawing us back to her more and
more. One time, on the spur of the moment, we jumped in
the truck with our fishing poles and tackle box, throwing
a few things to nibble on in a cooler, grabbed the camp

stove to make coffee and set off for a day's fishing on the river. After arriving at our favourite spot on the bank of the John Day River and casting in our lines, we found it hard to think of leaving for home.

"Let's just stay the night!" I said, realizing it was impracticable since we had neither tent, sleeping bag nor even a blanket! We had driven the little Nissan work truck so even that was not an option of making oneself comfortable inside to sleep!

"But we don't have anything to sleep on or in to stay warm," Darrell pointed out, all the while with a big grin on his face! "How and where exactly will we sleep?"

"We'll make do! I just am not ready to go home yet. Can't we stay?" I replied. Resourceful fellow that he is, Darrell started digging through the odds and ends in the back of the truck, coming up with an old tarp – none too clean I might add – that was just big enough for us to lie on part of it, flipping the rest over us as a cover. We snuggled together under the tarp, on the hard ground by the side of the truck, both of us agreeing we were crazy! It was a long, cold and very uncomfortable night, but we laughed about it the next morning, so glad we had thrown in the camp stove and makings for hot coffee! This impromptu stay had planted a seed in our mind. We loved this part of the country; it was drawing us here almost every weekend, yet neither of us voiced out loud what we were thinking.

Maybe that cold night, snuggled up in a tarp, was the catalyst for the change coming soon to our lives. Darrell worked hard through the week, I worked hard on the farm and when the weekend came it inevitably saw us driving off for a day or two fishing on the John Day River. On one such jaunt, right out of the blue, Darrell asked, "How would you like to live over here?"

"Are you serious?" I said, swiveling around in my seat

to look to see if he was joking, if he was just pulling my leg. "Yes, oh yes! I would love to live here!" A grin spread over Darrell's face and at that moment we both knew this was where we wanted to be. Bend was growing at quite a fast pace which was, of course, good for Darrell's business. However, Bend in 1991 did not seem to be the same friendly little town I had moved to in 1985 and definitely was not the same place as when Darrell came in the late 1970s! It was becoming a true city, making us both feel it was time to move on.

Once the thought had been put into words and we both knew we were of the same mind, the planning began. Where on earth did one start? We had so much to do! First was looking for a place to buy in the John Day country. We really liked the Spray and Kimberly areas on the river. Next, put our K-Barr farm on the market. To be prepared, at Darrell's little shop in Bend, we organized and consolidated all his electrical supplies, materials, equipment and such, so we could store unneeded household items there if required. The tasks were daunting! Not only that, but how were we going to afford to buy a place over on the river where we loved to fish? We were not exactly rolling in funds. Could we even find a suitable piece of land over there, and how difficult will it be to sell our place here in Bend? Were we doing the right thing? Yes, we were, we could feel it.

Darrell, now with a goal in mind, went to work with a vengeance. From early in the morning until dusk he worked, taking on every job he could. A real estate agent was retained and a price set on our K-Barr farm. Eventually, after much searching, we found 60 acres of land situated between Kimberly and Spray on the John Day River. Seemingly perfect for us, it was two and a half hours drive from Bend and an hour's drive from John Day, the closest actu-

al town of any size. The land lay alongside the John Day
River although was bisected by the main road. The fences
were in disrepair, few were even standing. The hay field on
the river side of the property was in sad shape and would
need a lot of work just to improve it as pasture. There was
however electricity on the property which ran down to the
irrigation pump, but no buildings of any kind, nothing!
"What do you think Rose? There's going to be a lot of work
to be done here. We would be starting from scratch again
… no home, no running water, nothing. Do you really
want to start all over again?" Darrell asked, putting his arm
around my shoulder. I think he saw the answer in my eyes
even before I said the words.
"I am not worried about the work. I love the place. We can
make a good life here, but how on earth could we afford
to even pay the down payment until we sell our farm in
Bend?" I spoke out loud the thought that was crossing
both our minds as we looked out at the land that lay before us knowing this was where we wanted to be.
"We will figure it out; after all, aren't you the one who is
always telling me to trust in Fate?" Darrell said with that
wonderful, warm grin of his.

Back in the late 1980s, Darrell had been one of the few
contractors who stuck to his guns and rode the economic
depression and high interest rate times through to the end.
When so many contractors literally picked up sticks and
moved in the middle of the night, leaving bills unpaid or
declaring bankruptcy to clear their huge debts, Darrell did
not. He battled on, determined to pay the bills many of the
general contractors had left him with. He may have had his
name in partnership with others on a piece of land here
or there, but his bottom line when we were first married
was seriously in the red! So how on earth could we afford
to buy more land without first selling our farm and home?
We had put every spare penny we had into paying off Del

Kennel, the fellow who was Darrell's partner at one time on the K-Barr property. We had no spare funds at all.

Yet Darrell was determined. The one thing he did have of some value, was old Chevy cars in various stages of restoration. There was a classic 1939 Chevy, the 1955 Handyman Wagon that was my project car, a couple of '57 Chevys Darrell had planned on restoring and finally there was his Winchester gun collection. Darrell loved old Winchester rifles and over the years had collected some dandy ones! Without a second thought, he sold the old cars as well as many of his rifles in order to come up with enough cash for the down payment on the John Day River land. The work would be hard, the sacrifices many but we had a dream, and we had a goal. The down payment was ultimately made and in July of 1991 the river land was ours. During the next few months, we arranged our lives around the farm in Bend and the land alongside the river. It was a huge adjustment. Our camper was moved to the Kimberly land and set up in the field near the power pole and irrigation pump down by the river. Little did I realize at the time that this was soon to become my home away from home.

As we began work improving the pasture and hay grounds, we decided it would make sense for me to stay in Kimberly a few days a week in order to fully irrigate the fields – there just was not enough time to do so over a weekend. This would help in preparing the land for eventually moving our livestock over in the not-too-distant future! So, while Darrell headed back to Bend on Sunday afternoon, I stayed on the river farm in the camper at Kimberly, working and irrigating the hay fields, fixing and building fences – eventually learning how to mow, rake and bale hay! Usually, I could get the field completely watered by Wednesday evening, then I could leave and drive back to Bend to help Darrell on the K-Barr farm. This also gave me chance to

catch up on my Darrell's Electric bookkeeping chore too!
Being away from each other, even for a few days of the
week, was so very, very hard. We constantly had to remind
ourselves it would not be forever. Little did we know there
would be a good few years of this sacrifice before the day
came when I no longer had to watch and weep as I saw
Darrell's work van head down the driveway and off to
Bend.

It was quite an experience for me, living part of the week
alone in our little camper by the river. Other than for a
short period of time before I met and married Darrell, I
have never lived on my own before. Of course, I was not
totally on my own as I had our dog Bear, our first Rottwei-
ler, with me. That is one thing I loved about Darrell, he
had no problem with us having a dog or any other pet! He
wasn't one for having cats in the house, but I could live
with that! After we lost Jasper, my golden retriever and
faithful pal, a lady I gave riding lessons to and good friend
of mine, gave me a black lab puppy after their bitch had
a fine litter. Emmy was a grand dog, a natural hunter and
fabulous gundog although a wee bit timid otherwise and
certainly not a guard dog! My being alone on the river really worried Darrell to no end. What I needed was a good
dog who would at least bark and warn me if anyone came
around. Thus, we got our first of many Rottweilers.

This was an exceedingly challenging time for Darrell and
me. Neither one of us could bear to be apart from the other yet we knew it had to be done. Our time alone, him in
Bend and me in Kimberly, was filled with work, work, work
and more work. For me it was getting up in the morning,
making a quick cup of tea in the camper before heading
into the field to change irrigation pipe. This was followed
by packing up the back of my little truck with barbed wire,
metal posts and other fencing supplies for a long day's

hard work repairing the old fence line on the other side of the road. A very necessary chore as one of these days soon we hoped to move our cattle over here. I like building fence but do not particularly like barbed wire! On the far side of the road, away from the river and green hay field, the balance of our land was hilly, dry and in places, very steep. There was nothing but deer trails to follow which meant lugging rolls of barbed wire and 6' metal T-posts up the steep slopes by hand. I became adept at stringing and repairing wire with the old-fashioned fence stretcher and fit as a fiddle from climbing the hills in the hot summer sun. One day, however, I did have a good scare, which brought to light the dangers of being on one's own with no neighbours in sight or hearing distance!

I was working on a particularly steep section of fence line in which the barbed wire was old, loose, fragile and very rusty. It definitely needed to be replaced. Darrell had given me one of his old leather tool belts on which I was able to hang my hammer, fencing pliers and it also had pockets, handy for fence staples and other odds and ends. Since much of this steep ground was rocky, the original old fence was kept upright using wooden stays cut from the myriad of juniper trees that dotted the hillside, the occasional rock crib adding support here and there. After splicing in some new barbed wire onto each of the four old rusty strands, I tightened the stands using the fence stretcher. Now came the tricky task of stapling the banjo-tight wires to the old wooden stays. On level ground this was an easy accomplishment, not so on a steep, slippery hillside! Reaching over the now tight barbed wire fence with my left arm, I proceeded to hold a staple in place, preparing to secure the wire to the post by hammering with my right hand. This is when disaster struck! The dry, rocky, slippery ground suddenly fell away beneath my feet. I found myself hanging from the barbed wire fence, a rusty but very sharp barb impaling the crook of my left arm, holding me tight as if I were in a trap!

The pain was excruciating, and blood was trickling from the crook of my arm all the way to my armpit! I was sprawled on my side by the fence, the fence itself the only thing preventing me from plummeting down the hillside, my left arm strung up on the fence above my head. Gritting my teeth, I tried to gain purchase with my feet, attempting in vain to stand up. Every move made the barb sink deeper into my arm, increasing the blood flow from a trickle to a steady stream. A sob escaped me. Now this was a fine mess I had gotten myself into! "Think Rose! You can't just lie here all day!" I scolded myself. Carefully I pulled my fencing pliers out of the tool pouch, slowly sliding my leg around until I felt a seemingly solid rock under my foot. Bracing against it, I gingerly tried to push my body up the slope enough so I could reach up with my right hand and cut the wire that had me impaled. Why had I done such a good job of tightening it? Finally, the pliers accomplished their job, the wire snapped and once freed, I slid a few feet down the slope, grasping my arm to staunch the blood.

Bear came from where I had commanded him to stay during the ordeal, snuggled up next to me, seeming to know I needed his comfort. Eventually, the bleeding stopped, so I carefully fixed the broken wire and on somewhat shaky legs, made my way down the hillside to the truck. I needed a fortifying cup of tea after that experience I can tell you! It took me quite a long while before I told Darrell of my ordeal, knowing it would put even more fear into him leaving me alone on the river when he had to head back to Bend. To this day I have a scar that reminds me of my hillside predicament. Looking back, I can almost laugh at what a picture I must have presented … hanging by one arm alone there on that steep, dusty hillside.

It was hard being by myself, but it made me grow as a person. I knew Darrell was working just as hard in Bend, harder in fact, since he was the main bread winner. As well as keeping his electrical contracting business going, he had all the farm chores to do when he arrived home from work at night. We did not have cell phones in those days and the evenings spent all alone were painfully hard for both of us. They say distance makes the heart grow fonder, well in our case it most certainly did! Occasionally I would need to stay in Kimberly for a fortnight or more at a time. Friday afternoon would arrive, and I would eagerly listen for the distinctive sound of Darrell's white work van. Watching for it to appear around the bend in the road, as it slowed down and turned onto the track leading down to the camper by the river, my heart filled with delight. We so enjoyed our time together on the weekends, but Sunday afternoon always rolled around far too soon. Darrell would reluctantly get ready to head back to Bend and it was always a tearful time for me. Realistically, we knew Darrell would have to keep his electrical contracting business going in Bend, even after we sold the K-Barr farm. There just was not enough work over here on the river to support us. I always pushed that thought from my mind.

That first season on the Kimberly farm was certainly a challenging one for me. I have never been someone who makes decisions easily. Maybe it was my upbringing, the fear of always making the wrong choice. Maybe it was just my nature, but whatever it was, I had – and still do – have a hard time coming to a decision about some things. This time on the river was to be my first experience of making hay all on my own. We had moved our haying equipment from K-Barr over to Kimberly in preparation for when we would finally sell the K-Barr farm and have to move lock, stock and barrel to our new home. The field by the river was starting to grow a nice stand of grass and alfalfa which, when cut and dried, would make dandy hay for our cows

and horses. Darrell was an expert farmer and had raised
and harvested hay for years. This season however, when
the hay was ready to be cut and harvested, he was busy
working over in Bend, so the task lay to me.

Haying can be a tricky affair sometimes. Knowing when to
cut it is not such a big chore other than picking a window
where the weather will cooperate and not rain as soon as
the crop is laid down! Then there is the raking and most
importantly of all, the baling of it. I was happy to do the
cutting and raking. There is something rewarding in seeing the tall standing crop mowed down into a flat swath as
you chug along on the tractor. Baling is something else. If
the crop is too damp when you bale it, you stand a chance
of the bales spontaneously combusting when they have
been stacked for a while as the internal heat builds to a
breaking point. Bale when the alfalfa crop is too dry, and
all the leaves are beaten off the stems, making the hay lose
a significant portion of its feed value. It has to be baled just
right!

There was no choice for it, the haying was up to me. Darrell, bless his heart, had utter faith I could handle it. The
hay had been cut and raked but Darrell had to head back
to Bend before it was ready to bale. I was going to have
to make the decision as to when the crop was ready. Daily
I checked the swaths just as Darrell had taught me, twist-
ing a handful of the stems to see how they felt, how they
looked. The weather seemed to be changing with clouds
starting to roll in on the day I finally made the decision
to bale. Thankfully the old baler chugged along; gobbling
up the windrow in front and spitting out perfectly formed
bales behind. Once the field was done, neat rows of rect-
angular bales lay just waiting to be picked up. The clouds
were still rolling in, but the rain thankfully was holding
off. After feeling proud of myself for doing such a tidy job,

I sure didn't want to see those bales rained on! We had an old bale wagon at the time – a wonderful thing when it was running right and a devil when it was not! The machine swiftly scooped up bales from the ground, forming them into a tidy package that could then be transported to the hay yard and neatly stacked, all without the tractor operator leaving their seat. Well, that is how it is supposed to work!

As anyone who has ever baled hay knows, it can be a hugely rewarding chore or a grossly frustrating one! When everything is working right it is incredibly fun. However, haying equipment, especially old, well-used haying equipment like we had – since it was all we could afford – was notoriously known to breakdown and always at a most crucial time. As I hooked up the tractor to the bale wagon, the clouds began to darken. No worries I thought, there was plenty of time to get these bales off the field and neatly stacked. The first few loads went off without a hitch. I was feeling pretty proud of my stacking abilities and the ease at which I had perfected the workings of the wagon, I felt like a pro! Maybe that was my downfall, for with still a couple ton of hay bales left to gather from the field, the bale wagon had other ideas and refused to cooperate!

Was that a drop of rain I felt on my head? Oh no! Another splattered on my arm. I couldn't bring myself to leave these remaining bales in the field; I had to get them to the stack! Abandoning the temperamental machinery, I decided to pick up the remaining bales by hand, loading them into the back of my little truck, driving them to the hay yard where I unloaded and stacked them by hand. It was exhausting work, but I finished up just as the rain started coming down in earnest. An overwhelming desire to see Darrell took hold of me. Closing up the camper, ushering Bear into the truck, I decided to head to Bend. The rain was coming down in sheets. I had heard of flash floods of course, but never truly believed they could be as fearsome and devastating as people made them out to be.

That storm however, made a believer of me! As I left our Kimberly farm and was heading towards Spray where I would veer off to Bend, the rain was so heavy I could barely see the road in front of me. The river was on my left and steep, barren hillsides to my right. Suddenly I saw rocks on the road, and mud, lots of mud! Water was cascading down the hillside, running across the road and into the river. I swung over into the other lane, avoiding the rocks – some could even be called boulders – and hurried on my way, nose inches from the windshield, peering out trying to see. I never was as glad to get out of a rainstorm as I was that day! Pulling into our driveway on K-Barr was the sweetest sense of homecoming I had had in a long while but being wrapped tight in Darrell's arms was even better.

Heading back to Kimberly a few days later we were able to see the destruction a true "gully washer" can do. Huge gouges had been made in what had once been small water pathways, the highway was damaged, trees, rocks and other debris had made islands in the river where there had been none. It sure reminded us how quickly Mother Nature can enforce her will on the land, and how truly awesome is her power!

Chapter 23.

1991 was coming to a close. Thanksgiving was approaching and still our K-Barr farm had not sold. The land in Kimberly was left to fend for itself through the winter, as we could not even think of moving over there until we sold the K-Barr farm. Darrell was still as busy as ever with his electrical work, which of course, we were certainly grateful. Our little meat business was thriving and since it was close to Thanksgiving, that meant the turkeys we had raised for meat customers were in need of dispatching. This year there were 12 that needed to be killed, plucked, processed and delivered in time to grace the Thanksgiving tables of our patrons.

Dispatching and butchering fowl is not my most favourite task! I would rather do a beef or a few pigs instead any day of the week! However, they had to be done. Darrell, feeling terrible he could not be there to help me, left for work – since Thanksgiving is always on a Thursday I dispatch turkeys on Monday, delivering them on Tuesday so they are nice and fresh for the holiday feast. I had developed a handy routine when doing so many turkeys at a time. It entailed dispatching about four of them at a time – I will not go into details right now for those readers of a sensitive nature. Dispatching was quickly followed by scalding the birds then promptly hanging them up to make plucking easier. It was a busy time and not one where one would want visitors popping in unannounced. Yet that is exactly what happened!

Darrell had made it very clear to our real estate agent that she must call in advance to set up a viewing appointment when she had a prospective buyer. So, imagine my surprise when I saw a car coming down the driveway towards me. Pulling to a stop a few feet from the end of the shop, our realtor, in smart skirt, jacket and high heels, alighting from the car followed by another equally well-dressed lady and gentleman! There I stood, blood on my hands in an old holey sweatshirt, my feet encased in muddy wellies. Four half plucked turkeys were strung up in the entrance to the shop, a bucket of turkey feathers and guts sat beside me while an additional four very dead turkeys lay on the ground waiting their turn in the scalding pot! I was not amused at their unanticipated arrival, but the looks of astonishment on the faces of the lady and gentlemen were priceless!

Breaking the awkward silence, the realtor introduced me to her clients. Wiping my hands on my trouser legs I said, "I won't shake your hands." Then turning to our realtor, who obviously realized she had made a blunder in not calling ahead of time, said in my most dignified voice, "I had no idea you would be coming by today. I am afraid you will have to show yourselves around as Darrell isn't here and this is a job I can't stop." Regaining her composure, the real estate lady smiled and turning to her clients, led them away from me and the scene of butchery. I was furious! What sort of impression did it give of the place? I had not had a chance to tidy up inside our home, even though it was not dirty by any means, but I knew there were breakfast dishes in the sink and the floor could have done with a wash. They soon left with the briefest of goodbyes and I continued with my work. Those folks obviously decided the place was not what they were looking for! When Darrell heard what had happened, he telephoned our agent and there was no doubt he made it clear from now on there would be no exception to the appointment rule!

Thinking we wouldn't hear from her for a while, it took us by surprise when she called, asking if she could bring a couple of clients out to look at the farm. The catch was it would have to be on Thanksgiving Day since the people were flying home the following morning. Darrell and I had no special plans, no family coming over, so it was fine with us. Now in our little home, we had a wood stove as well as a wood cookstove in the main living quarters. Since I primarily cooked on the wood cookstove, we had never actually installed the electric cooker in the kitchen, although Darrell had wired in a range plug. I was not a fan of cooking on an electric stove, so it resided, of all places, in the bathroom! I was making pies and bread in the wood cooker oven so had popped our whopper turkey in the electric stove oven. The delicious smell of roasting bird filled the house, albeit coming from the bathroom!

Imagine the surprise on the faces of the lady and gentleman who accompanied our agent, when they entered the apartment and discovered the delightful smell of roasting bird was coming from none other than the bathroom! As the gentleman said, that was the best smelling bathroom he had ever been in! They strolled through the house, thrilled to see me cooking dinner on the old cookstove. My old clawfoot bathtub had them exclaiming in delight. Leaving the warmth of the house, they headed out to wander around the farmyard and outbuildings, returning in a while to ask numerous questions before taking their leave. Darrell and I thought they seemed interested in the property, but it was going to take a very special buyer to want to live in a small apartment in the end of a metal shop instead of a large, luxurious house!

Putting them out of mind we started making plans for the coming year. Shortly after Thanksgiving we took a jaunt over to our Kimberly property with the idea of harvesting a couple of deer, as we had tags for the area. My father was passing through Bend on his way back home from Arizona and offered to stay at the K-Barr farm for a couple of days

while we were gone. We gladly took him up on his offer
and prepared to leave. It was chilly with a slight covering of
snow on the ground, perfect hunting weather. The thought
of staying in our camper was exciting since we had not
been out that way for a good while. Since buying the land,
we had become friends with our neighbours, Son and Lois
Hill, an elderly couple, who lived just up the river from our
property. It had become a daily indulgence for me when
I was living in the camper earlier in the year, to pop in to
see them for a cup of tea and chat. They were good about
keeping an eye on the place for us, and we always let them
know when we would be coming over for a few days.

After getting ourselves settled in the camper, we were
about to head out hunting when Son Hill came rattling
across the field in his old work truck. Jumping out he told
us he had just got a call from my father, apparently the real
estate agent had called him and said the people who came
to look at the farm on Thanksgiving wanted to buy it! We
had left the Hill's telephone number with my father in case
of an emergency. Thanking Son for delivering the message,
we quickly loaded our things back into the truck, locked
up the camper and headed back to Bend.

What great news! Within a couple of days my father headed home to Vancouver while we completed the deal on
our farm. Apparently, the thought of the old wood cookstove and the claw foot bathtub had sealed the deal for
the future owners of our K-Barr farm! Then it hit us. The
place would close a little after New Year! Between now and
then we had all our belongings to pack up, animals to find
a temporary home for, farm equipment and other large
things to move over to Kimberly. What an awful time to
have to do this!

Thank goodness for good friends! Arrangements were

made to keep our cows and horses in Redmond with friends Val and Mike, with us heading over to their place once a day to feed. Numerous trips transpired between Bend and Kimberly as we shuttled our farm equipment, water tanks, gates, corral panels and other big items over there on the snowy roads. Thankfully Darrell's shop and office in Bend was actually an old house, only a couple of doors down from our friends', the Cloughs. It took no time at all to move all the electrical supplies into the old garage adjacent to the house, effectively clearing out a couple of rooms in the back for us to move into. The Cloughs not only had their design studio, but also their mini-storage facility. This was perfect! A unit was rented in preparation for moving our entire household belongings into after the holidays – goodness knows when we would be settled enough to bring them to Kimberly! We decided to wait on packing up any of our household things until after Christmas as Darrell had come up with a brilliant idea.

Since this would be the last Christmas spent in our cozy K-Barr home and, as my father had decided to return to Vancouver instead of staying in sunny Arizona, why not invite him down to share the holidays with us? To save the long drive to Bend in what could be very inclement weather, we would fly him from Vancouver, B.C. to our local airport in Redmond. I immediately called him, telling him how much we would love to have him come and visit for this, our last Christmas at our K-Barr farm. He seemed thrilled and excited at the idea. Plans were made and we eagerly purchased the round-trip airline ticket as his Christmas treat.

It truly seemed as if our lives were on a happy track. Would there be challenges ahead? Naturally, for we knew there was no way Darrell could close the shop in Bend, business was booming, and one had to make hay while the sun shined. Putting the thought that there would be many days ahead when we would be apart, we lived in the moment. Slowly, slowly we were moving towards our goal of living our life in the John Day valley. Always a believer in Fate, I had no worries that everything would work out. Besides, months lay ahead of us before we had to face the challenges of living 150 miles apart.

We would enjoy this last Christmas in the little home we had built ourselves. My father be here to enjoy the holidays with us, the thought giving me much comfort. Soon, Darrell and I would find our lives once again changing and evolving but right now, things were perfect, what more could we ask for!

Chapter 24.

It was going to be a grand Christmas. I would have my father here for the holidays, all the way through to the New Year. I could see us baking and decorating and making this a really traditional English Christmas celebration! Darrell would still have to head off to work for a while each day, but even he was looking forward to having my father join us for the holidays. Days passed and snow came, building up on the roads and turning the fields into a smooth, sparkling expanse of white.

The airline tickets were purchased and sent up to Vancouver. Frequent telephone calls were made between my father and me and then the day finally arrived when we went to pick him up at our local airport. Sitting beside Darrell in the truck, excitement and yes, some apprehension filled me as we drove through the deepening snow from our farm to the airport. Excitement because we were going to be telling my father our plans to make him a special place to stay on our farm in Kimberly, apprehension because I always felt insecure around my father. It always seemed no matter what I did it was never quite good enough. I reached across the seat and took Darrell's hand, feeling comforted as his warm fingers wrapped around mine. All would be well. If only I could foresee the future, I would know this was not to be the case.

The drive from Bend to Redmond seemed to take longer than usual. We had left in plenty of time to pick my father up at the Redmond airport for his Christmas stay and Darrell was an excellent driver in the snow. When winter snows hit Bend, the road department kept Bend's main thoroughfare – highway 97 – drivable by plowing the road and pushing the excess snow up into a high berm in the center of the highway. Cuts made here and there in this snow berm allowed vehicles to turn into malls and other businesses with ease. It was a winter wonderland, but the icy roads could be treacherous!

Arriving at the airport terminal, we waited in the lobby area. Soon passengers from the newly arrived plane started trickling through the doors, to be eagerly met by family and friends. There was my father, coming through the door, bundled up in a nice sheepskin coat but, instead of the big smile I expected to see on his face, his expression was dour. My heart dropped, just knowing something had happened to put him out of sorts.

Dashing over to give him a hug and a kiss on the cheek my "Hello daddy!" was greeted by a gruff reply. After shaking Darrell's hand and giving him a slightly warmer greeting, we headed towards the baggage claim area. Apparently, the flight from Vancouver down to Redmond was not smooth sailing for my father. The journey had entailed a flight from Vancouver to Portland followed by the trip on the small plane to Redmond. There had been some slight delays, typical for this time of year, yet despite it all he was here safe and sound. However never one to grumble quietly, my father proceeded to expound his displeasure at the trip in a rather loud cantankerous voice as was his wont. Gathering up his single bag from the baggage roundabout, we headed out into the cold snowy parking lot eager to be on our way home – at least Darrell and I were!

The drive was filled with small talk and all of us were glad when we arrived home. Since our little home in the end of the shop only had the one bedroom, my father would be sleeping on the settee, well plied with blankets and warmed by the wood stove. This arrangement seemed to suit him just fine and we settled in for what I sincerely hoped would be a good visit despite the inauspicious beginning.

After a nice meal, we settled in for the night. The carpet of snow outside made for the perfect Christmas atmosphere, the tree in the corner of the front room gently scenting the house with the tang of pine was the final touch. Early the following morning, with just two days to go before Christmas Day, Darrell had to pop into town for a few hours, wrapping up a spot of work before taking a couple of days off for the holidays. After he left, I stoked the fire and made a good, strong cup of tea for my father, who was awake but still huddled under his blankets.

"How did you sleep daddy?" I asked as I handed him his tea, already noticing the disgruntled look on his face as he took the cup from my hand.

"Could have been better," was his somewhat morose reply. Deciding I needed to let him drink his tea in peace, I bundled up in warm coat and wellies before heading outside for morning feeding chores.

"I'll be back in a bit. I'm just going to get everyone fed and watered. We can have breakfast when I get back." Perhaps my father would be in a slightly better mood when I got back to the house. Something was obviously wrong, and as has always been the case, I felt it must be something I had done or said which upset the apple cart. How I wished Darrell were still at home!

It is so peaceful to be outside on a brisk snowy morning, throwing sweet smelling hay to the horses that nicker at you as they look expectantly over their stall doors when you enter the barn. Nothing but the quiet munching of contented equines breaks the morning stillness. Yet I was procrastinating, prolonging the morning chores. Time to get back to the house to make more tea and a spot of breakfast for my father, counting the few hours before Darrell would be home. I don't know why I should have felt so uneasy, why I felt such a deep feeling of foreboding, but I did. Better face whatever was niggling at me! Maybe

I was just imagining my father was out of sorts. Maybe had just "got up on the wrong side of the bed," as we used to say. After all, hadn't he been really excited about coming to visit for the holidays? What on earth could have changed between him leaving Vancouver and arriving here? Surely the inconvenience of a delay at the airport could not have set him off. Oh well, better see if a good cup of tea had sweetened his disposition!

As soon as I opened the door from the shop to the house I knew things had not changed; indeed they had gone from bad to worse. The air inside our little apartment was blue with cigarette smoke and there was my father, sitting on the settee, puffing away like a chimney. My heart sank. First of all, he was not supposed to be smoking – according to what he said his doctor had told him – and secondly, he knew neither Darrell nor I had the habit and as such did not allow smoking in our home. Yet here he was, blatantly puffing away. Not only that, but he sat on the edge of the settee, virtually buck naked except for a very brief – and I mean brief! – pair of red underpants! This is how he always used to wander around the house of a morning when I was a little girl, but now I certainly did not appreciate his attire at all!

I am sure there are many daughters out there who would have said, "For goodness' sake get some clothes on, father, and put that cigarette out!" Did I do that? Of course not! In front of my father, I was no longer a married woman of 28 years old, in her own home, but once again a mindful, timid little girl. Instead of saying what I should have said, I went around opening wide every window in the house. In no time at all, cozy warmth was replaced by frigid cold as a wintery breeze swept through the rooms, dissipating the smoke but bringing an arctic chill in its place. My father merely glared at me while he wrapped blankets around his shoulders, finally voicing his malcontent.

Angrily stubbing his cigarette out, he proceeded to mumble and grumble about the inconvenience of us bringing him down to visit for Christmas.

"I had plans you know." He stated belligerently.

"What do you mean, daddy? I thought you were really excited about coming down to see us for Christmas!" My heart was thumping, and I could feel tears prickling my eyes.

"Well, you could have asked me what I wanted instead of just saying you were bringing me here for Christmas. I had plans. Dances I wanted to go to, friends to see and other important things to do. You didn't consider that did you?" He glared at me, but I could not meet his eyes, I was that little girl in trouble again.

"But why didn't you tell us you didn't want to come! We would have understood. We thought you wanted to visit, that it would be a nice thing to have you here for Christmas!" I was on the verge of tears but was somewhat amazed to realize I also felt anger rising in me. We had spent a good bit of money, money we did not have in abundance, in order to fly my father down for the holidays. Now here he was telling me he did not want to be here.

As the anger inside me grew, I found myself finally feeling brave enough to speak my mind as he went to light up yet another cigarette.

"This is my house, daddy, and there will be no smoking in it!" That seemed to infuriate him, that I had the audacity to tell him what he could and could not do.

"What did you just say to me?" he said, his voice taking on that tone which I was so familiar with whenever I was in trouble. "You dare to tell me I can't smoke when I want to? Don't you ever talk that way to me!" I felt I had crossed a line. Had I just had the nerve to speak back to my father?

He stood up, shrugging off the blankets around his shoulders, pulling on his trousers that lay nearby. Then, before I knew it, he was standing in front of me.

"I had plans for this Christmas," he went on again, pulling on his socks and shirt. "Now they are all messed up because of you! I wish I had never got on that plane!" The anger built inside me, recalling all the times I had held my tongue in the past. Without thinking, I blurted out,

"I wish you had never come either!" At that moment, just as my father raised his hand to slap my face for answering him back in such a cheeky way, Darrell walked through the door.

The look on Darrell's face is one I shall never, ever forget. He took in the scene in a flash and was immediately by my side, his hand on my arm. Seldom in my life had I seen my father look scared, but in that moment he did, he knew he had crossed a line. Darrell looked down into his face, his voice controlled yet menacing.

"Don't you ever think of raising your hand to my wife! If you do, it will be the last thing you ever do!" I was in tears but with Darrell by my side I felt safe. My father quickly regained his composure, turning to me he said,

"I am leaving. I am going back home. Take me to the airport right now." It took no time at all for him to gather his belongings and we found ourselves in the truck heading towards Bend on the snow-covered roads. Little was said between us, the atmosphere thick enough you could cut it with a knife! It was going to be a long and uncomfortable trip to the airport.

As we entered Bend and turned onto the main road that would take us to Redmond and the airport, my father suddenly declared he wanted to get out.

"You can't get out here daddy, we are not even close to the airport. It's miles away in the next town! There are no busses in Bend you know."

"Let me out here! Right now. I'll walk," he angrily replied, I am sure counting on me to protest and reason with him. That is how it had always been, he would make a stand and I would capitulate, then after much crying and promising to do better, he would finally bestow his forgiveness on me. Once again, the old pattern was playing out. However, he had not taken into account Darrell who had stoically driven from our farm into Bend without saying a word to my father.

"Let me out here. Right here, right now!" my father repeated. Suddenly, the truck came to a stop. Darrell got out and coming around to the curbside, effortlessly lifted my father's suitcase out of the bed of the truck, opened the passenger door and without a word, placed my father's bag on the snowy sidewalk. Looking once at me, almost in disbelief, my father climbed out of the truck, grabbed his bag and started walking down the street without looking back. I am sure he was expecting me to run after him, begging him to get back in the truck, telling him I was sorry. But it did not happen. For once, someone had called his bluff.

Resolutely, Darrell shut the passenger door, walked back around the truck, and climbed in beside me. Without a word he put his arm around my shoulders as he drove off, turning the truck around towards home. My heart felt broken. What would my father do? What had I done! Tears filled my eyes and the crushing feeling of guilt, of being at fault, threatened to overwhelm me. Yet the weight of Darrell's arm on my shoulders gave me comfort, I could feel his love surrounding me. He had protected me in a way no one else had ever done. He was my rock. As he drove us home, he told me not to be worried about my father for when he stopped the truck it was right beside a motel on the main strip in town. My father, he assured me, could take care of himself.

Weak and shaky, still feeling guilty, I let Darrell lead me into our home where he stoked up the fire and put the kettle on for tea. Later that night as we sat snuggled side by side on the settee, we talked. I told him all my fears about my father, ingrained over the years, while he listened, keeping me wrapped tight in his arms. We were alone that Christmas of 1991, just the two of us celebrating the holiday. My father made it back home, somehow finagling the airlines into changing his return ticket for an earlier flight date with no problem. It was weeks before we corresponded, me expecting a barrage of anger from him; instead, he acted as if nothing untoward had happened. Yet something had changed between us. I think he realized I was no longer his little, obedient girl, the Rose he could intimidate and frighten. No, that Rose was gone. I was blossoming, for now I had a husband who would help me stand up to my father, to anyone! I had someone strong beside me, supporting and encouraging me, a true soulmate and partner for life.

Chapter 25.

They say distance makes the heart grow fonder; well, the coming years would test that long-standing adage to the core! By March of 1992, our trusty old camper, set up by the side of the river under some big old trees, was our Kimberly home. The K-Barr place was behind us and new roads lay ahead.

Darrell was kept busy working in Bend. Living in our little house which served as accommodation as well as the business shop for Darrell's Electric during the week, he began the first of many years of travelling back and forth between the city and our river land at Kimberly. It was imperative Darrell's Electric remained in Bend as that is where the work was, and it fell on Darrell's shoulders to provide for our livelihood. The sacrifice of being apart for days on end would be worth it we kept telling ourselves.

Friday afternoon would roll around and I would find myself staring up at the highway, listening and waiting impatiently for first the sound then the sight of Darrell's work truck. Watching for it to round the bend, slowing down to turn down the bumpy track leading to our camper. Tears would fill my eyes as we hugged and kissed, for even being apart a mere five days seemed an eternity! Darrell always brought brownies from Safeway home with him, which we would devour with our morning tea and coffee the following day. Usually, a bucket of fried chicken picked up as he left Prineville on Friday night was dinner, but the rest of our meals were cooked in the camper on our little gas stove.

Later, as we lay snuggled side by side in the cramped sleeping area of the camper, we would plan the coming weekend's work and what needed to be completed in the coming week. There was so much to be done! Thankfully, the preparations made before our K-Barr farm sold had paid off. All our cows and horses were settled on our river farm, corrals were up, and life had assumed a steady routine. Now we could start thinking of building our new home; it was time. Never a fan of cold water, taking my baths in the chilly John Day River in early March was not something I would miss at all!

With the Clough's designing expertise, a house plan was drawn up. Nothing fancy, just a simple one-story affair that would fit our needs perfectly. Darrell eventually bought a small Cat dozer to help in the clearing of brush from the land. My goodness did that thing scare the daylights out of me at times! I would watch as Darrell headed up and down slopes, working the handles frantically to keep the thing running straight and true. Every now and then when the blade hit a particularly stubborn rock, the back end of the little dozer would come off the ground, the wobbly seat threatening to buck Darrell off! I cannot count the number of times my heart was in my throat! That was one piece of farm equipment I had no desire to mess around with, cantankerous thing that it was!

Finally, we were ready to get cracking on the actual building our new home and all the necessary permits obtained. Darrell hired a wonderful old gentleman, Alton McBride, to come and make a good driveway up to the house site and level out the plot for the foundation. His big dozer made short work of the job and before long the foundation of our new home was done. The framing could begin. One of the convenient things about Darrell being an electrical contractor was his ability to trade his work for that of other contractors. So it was we were able to get the rough plumbing and sheet rocking all done on the barter system! A building contractor Darrell worked with agreed to come over and help us get our home framed up in early April. All the material was delivered, we were ready to go.

Gary Bendix arrived, and we planned out the following day's work as we huddled that night around the fire built between our camper and the trailer Gary would live in for the next few days. It was freezing! Little did we know the temperature would soar into the low one-hundred-degree range just a couple of days later, making us wish for those cooler temperatures to return! Now Darrell is a grand carpenter, in fact he can turn his hand to just about anything; however, having someone whose job day in and day out was framing houses made our job that much easier. In seven days, the house was framed up, walls, roof and even the windows were in. Not bad for three people working together! After Gary left, Darrell and I sat on the bluff overlooking a bend in the John Day River. We truly felt as if we had found our dream spot to live. With hard work and the sacrifice of spending days apart, our life in the John Day country was just beginning and we felt ready for any challenges ahead.

Over the next couple of months, our house slowly became a home. While Darrell was working in Bend, I painted walls and stained cabinet wood and trim. Another one of Darrell's friends had done the rough plumbing for us in the house and I decided to take on the task of the finish work. Thoroughly enjoying the task of hooking up taps and setting sinks, we even found an old claw foot bathtub that sat below a large window taking pride of place in the bathroom. I always was – and still am - an aficionado of a long hot soak in a tub! Not someone himself who enjoyed soaking in hot water, a nice big shower stall was installed for Darrell. Finally, we found a lovely old wood cookstove and our home was complete. Well, almost!

On the exterior of the house, we used T1-11 siding then added strips of 1" wood so it would resemble the old-fashioned board and batt siding seen on old buildings. Normally I am a very conservative person when it comes to paint colours but wanted to do something "creative" on the exterior of our new home. Going through paint chip cards I thought I had picked the perfect colour combinations, a rich burgundy for the wood trim around the doors and windows and a nice warm beige colour for the main body of the house. Yes, that would look smart! Darrell, bless his heart, had utter faith in my choice. So, paint was purchased and while Darrell was working in Bend I got cracking and soon had the house painting done. Hmmm… somehow that nice beige paint looked a little different once it was on and dried.

Friday evening arrived and as always, I was on pins and needles listening for the sound of the old white van that would tell me Darrell was almost home. Would this impatient longing to see him ever wane I wondered? There it was, the sound of the engine roaring around the bend in the road then slowing down to make the turn into our driveway. Would he like the paint job on the house? Grinning from ear to ear I waited on the deck for the van to pull up. As he climbed out of the seat, I could see him staring up at the house as I ran up to him. Wrapping me in his arms and giving me a warm hug, he said, "It's pink!" My bubble burst.

"No, it's not pink!" I replied, "It's a beigy tan."

"Rose, from the road the house is pink! Really, it ´ pink!" He said with a grin.

"Never! Let's go look." So, we walked hand i´ up the driveway to the road and oh my goodne´ admit, in a certain light, looking at it from the´ indeed have a pinkish tint to it. That was n´ colour looked on the paint chip card in t´

for my creative side. We could either live with it or repaint it a good old simple grey… at least the burgundy trim around the windows and doors looked good! We decided to live with it for now.

The weekends were so brief. Before we knew it, Darrell was packing up his van ready to make the trip back to Bend for the coming week's work. This never, ever was easy. Tears would flow as we hugged each other tight. Then, watching as Darrell drove off down the driveway, we would wave like mad to each other until the van made the turn onto the main road and disappeared out of sight. Even when the van was out of sight I would still stand, waiting and listening for the final "toot toot!" of the horn which always made the tears flow even more.

How hard it was to be apart from the one you loved. How much I had to fight the urge to just sit down and let the sadness consume me. Bear would come and thrust his head under my arm, leaning his body against me as if he knew the pain I was in. Pulling myself together, I thought about the coming weeks' worth of chores on the agenda. This separation was a necessary evil we would tell ourselves, a way to get ahead, to build our future over here on the river. Oh, it was easy to say but so very, very hard to live through.

Daily chores kept my mind busy. Down below the house at the edge of our big field, we had set up pipe corrals and pens for the horses beside what would eventually be our garden plot. A low building was built to serve as chicken coop, storage area and future pig house. Fenced off from he remainder of the field, this area was our "barnyard." ur land was bisected by the main road, Highway 19, that 1 alongside the John Day River from Service Creek down ugh Kimberly and onwards. Between the highway and the river sat our house on the bluff overlooking a bend in the river and the irrigated hay field below. Our cows, the few that we had, grazed the hillside part of our property on the north side of the road until being moved into the hay fields once the native grasses started drying up and the main hay crop had been harvested from the land.

I love changing irrigation pipe! There is something so rewarding about seeing a field greening up almost before your eyes as the water from the river and the warmth of the sunshine encourages the grass to grow! The steady sound of the sprinkler heads ticking round, spewing their arcs of water in perfect circles. Well, that is when everything is working perfectly of course! Like most things to do with farming, there are the occasional glitches. Nothing is more frustrating than when a sprinkler head breaks loose, and a gusher of water shoots nearly 30 feet in the air like the geyser Old Faithful in full form! Or when you add those additional sections of pipe to your line, open the valve and discover a large sage rat had crept unawares into one of the pipes.

How do you know? Well, for those not familiar with the intricacies of farm irrigation pipe, let me first give you a brief overview. In a typical field, you have a mainline pipe, which is usually 4 to 6 inches or more in diameter and runs from the irrigation pump across your field. Every 40 feet or so along this main pipe will be a valve head which allows one to run lateral lines of smaller diameter pipe out into the field. These lateral lines are typically 3-inch diameter pipe, each 20 feet long. Each of these 20-foot sections has a riser – normally a 1-inch pipe about 12 or more inches high – with the sprinkler head mounted on the top. A nozzle on the sprinkler head controls the amount of water said sprinkler emits. Each sprinkler covers a circle of approximately 30-foot diameter. The nozzle on the sprinkler head is typically 1/8" to 3/16" in diameter. The force of the water coming down these pipes is quite tremendous as one can be running a quarter mile or more of pipe at one time. Got the picture?

So back to the sage rat in the pipe. You normally never see those sneaky little rodents entering the next length of pipe you are adding to your line. So you have no idea one is in there until you hook that last section of pipe on and attach the plug in the end and traipse back to the main valve to turn the water on, filling the pipe to the brim and firing the sprinklers up. Drat! That last sprinkler head is plugged! Grabbing the ever-present piece of baling wire wrapped conveniently around one of the other risers, you tromp down the line, narrowly avoiding getting sprayed by numerous forceful jets of water, to the plugged sprinkler nozzle. Forcing the wire down the narrow hole to loosen whatever is plugging it up, that is when you realize it is not a seed or pebble or chunk of grass that is causing the blockage. No indeed! It was something far more gruesome! A sage rat – or what was left of a sage rat – is being forced, piece by piece, through that little opening. I will leave it up to your imagination what a mess there is!

Yes, the joys of changing pipe! Add onto that the fact that on scorching hot summer days, rattlesnakes often like to lay stretched out alongside the cool irrigation pipe, quite unseen when the grass and alfalfa is as high as one's knee. Thank goodness I like snakes! Pipe changing is a twice a day chore that, added onto feeding horses, checking fence, building fence, working on the house kept me pretty busy for the most part. Yet my life was not all work. There was usually time to pop down the road to the Hill's farm where Lois Hill would put the kettle on for a cup of tea and a chat. Sometimes I would help these old folks out by sad-dling up Luke and heading off up the draw into the rimrock country above to look for some of their wayward cows that had a tendency to stray. After all, that is what neighbours do, help each other out in times of need. Thankfully I had a great partner in Luke as he sure got me out of many a tight spot up there when riding all alone after cows that were wild and wooly! Many is the time I gave him a loose rein while I grabbed mane and trusted to his surefootedness to get us out of a pickle!

Sometimes, the longing to see Darrell would win out over chores and I would jump in the little Chevy S-10 pickup, trusty Bear dog by my side, and zoom off to Bend. It was hard to wait for the weekend to arrive. What joy it was to see the big smile on Darrell's face when I pulled up to the curb in front of the office. How good his arms felt as they wrapped me in a tight embrace. Sometimes one just has to be with the love of your life and to heck with the work waiting at home! What sacrifices we made in those days in order to live where we wanted to live. How hard it was to be apart but how sweet when we were together.

Chapter 26.

The tail end of 1993 was rolling around and six years into our marriage, here we were, just as in love as ever! Could our life be more perfect? Absolutely! For starters, if waving a magic wand could make all our bills and financial challenges disappear, we would do it in a flash. Not for the pleasure of having no bills to speak of, but instead knowing it would mean Darrell and I could be together all the time. No more enduring the heartache of seeing his van heading down our driveway on a Sunday afternoon as he headed back to Bend, no more listening for that last "toot, toot!" of his horn as he disappeared around the corner.

Our farm was flourishing as was Darrell's electrical contracting business in Bend. Instead of building the shop back up to how it was in the 1980s, when Darrell's Electric, Inc. was one of the largest such establishments in Bend, he was content to work hard on the jobsites himself with only a couple of additional employees. There were select contractors he worked for who mainly built custom homes and the occasional commercial building. Darrell worked hard wiring houses all week only to come home to the farm and work just as hard on our own building projects! What a chap!

On the home front, our farm was growing. Darrell had never yet found a horse to replace his great old partner Kook, who passed away at the ripe old age of 30 and lay buried on our K-Barr farm, but we still had Luke, Smokey and Charro. Along with our modest herd of beef cows, was Mandy the Holstein milk cow as well as Milly and Tilly our two Yorkshire pigs. Chickens and turkeys were housed in the low building we built down by the large vegetable garden and Bear dog kept all in check. The hay fields flourished. Yes, life was good.

Over the past couple of years, what at first had been a rather strained relationship with Darrell's daughters, Terresa and Susan, had flourished into good friendships. Susan, her husband Jeff and our little grandson Jesse, made frequent visits to the farm and this had made the friendship between us grow even more. Thus, when the dark clouds began forming on the horizon, I found a port in the storm in that friendship.

Ever since what I refer to as the Christmas Debacle, my father and I resumed a tenuous relationship. For me, I felt I had grown and was a firmly established independent woman with a wonderful husband by her side. I tried to tell myself my father finally understood this although might never admit it – at least to me! Slowly we began writing back and forth to each other, the correspondence always warm and polite, nothing suggesting anything untoward had occurred between us. I wrote about my daily life on the farm, he about his sojourns to various dance halls with his numerous lady friends, although one had obviously become his favourite partner. Just when I thought old wounds were healing, the advertisements began to arrive, neatly cut out of his local newspaper and tucked between the folded notepaper.

It did not immediately dawn on me why my father would send such cuttings then, reading between the lines of his letter, it hit me. At first, I thought he was just showing me what farms and land cost up in the Okanagan Valley of British Columbia. Circled in red pen and cut from the real estate sales page of his local newspaper, were pictures of beautiful houses nestled amongst trees. Descriptions of well-tended farms with orchards, barns, horse paddocks and fields. Then I began to understand. He wanted me back and this was his way of trying to coax me away from

Darrell. He would buy me a farm ... in Canada.

"Can you believe he would try to bribe me to leave you by buying me a farm in the Okanagan?" I asked Darrell, waving the letter in one hand and the advertisement in the other. "How could he even suggest such a thing!" My temper was getting the better of me as I stormed around the kitchen.

"Rose, you know what your dad is like," Darrell said as he calmly sat at our kitchen table watching me. "He'll do anything and say anything to get you back. To him you will always be his little girl and no matter who you are married to, that will always be a thorn in his side."

"I know, but to try to get me to leave you. How could he do such a thing? Hasn't he realized that you are the one I want to be with?" Getting up from the table, Darrell wrapped his arms around me as the tears began to fill my eyes.

"He loves you, Rose."

"I know that, but I could never, ever leave you. He should know that by now. You are my life!" In Darrell's arms I felt safe. It might be hard to imagine but getting those snippets of newspaper from my father scared me. Although he was miles and miles away, I could feel his presence, almost see him smiling as if he was enjoying my discomfort. No, I must put thoughts like that out of my head! I would tell myself, over and over and over again. He could not hurt me now. Replying to his letters, I studiously avoided any mention of the enclosures. He must have got the message as his tack changed, and in a way that had my mind in a whirl.

Back when we lived on our K-Barr farm in Bend, my father had hinted he had a problem which was why his doctor had told him to stop smoking. Never actually coming out and saying he had cancer, the seed had been planted in my mind. When we resumed our correspondence after the Christmas Debacle, more and more hints of his deteriorating medical condition would surface in his letters and telephone calls. Problem was, my father had a rich history of "swinging the lead," playing on one's sympathies by suggesting dire illness which invariably turned out to be nothing at all. He did have a heart condition but even that was something he had used to his advantage on several occasions. This crying wolf, though, was about to catch up to him.

When he first began openly mentioning having lung cancer, I did not believe him. Too many past stories that turned out to be false had made me a sceptic. I admit, I was a bit blasé. When he would talk about how sick he was one minute then regale me with his latest stories of square-dancing escapades and trips down to Mesa with friends, it was hard to see him as really being ill. Was this just another ploy to get me to go back to Vancouver? Well, if it was, it wasn't going to work! Then, the letters and calls started coming more and more frequently.

"Rose, I am not doing well. The doctor thinks the cancer is spreading" my father said in a telephone call to me one day. "He thinks I might not have long to live." I could hear him puffing away on a cigarette as he spoke.

"Daddy, are you smoking? I can hear you smoking!" How could he still be smoking if he truly had lung cancer?

"To hell with what the doctor says about me stopping smoking! If I am going to die, what does it matter? I miss you, Rose. Can't you come up for a visit? I know Jenny would love to see you." So, Jenny, his longtime dance partner was still with him, that's good I thought.

"I miss you too, daddy, but I can't get away from the farm right now. Who is your doctor? Can I talk to him?" Why was it I still did not believe what he was telling me?

"Doctor Cook. A nice chap. I have been seeing him

for a while now. I can get him to ring you." We chatted for a few more minutes then said our bye-byes before hanging up.

As I sat there by the 'phone, doubts began to creep into my mind. Was I wrong? Did my father really have cancer and was it truly as bad as he made it out to be? Would he really get his doctor to call me and could I even trust what the doctor said was true? After all, hadn't I been fooled by a doctor in the past? Slowly, insidiously, guilt crept up on me. What sort of a daughter am I? I asked myself. What if daddy really is sick? If only Darrell was home, but he was over in Bend, working. I would tell him about my father's call tonight when we called each other to share the day's news. Oh, how I wished he was here with me now!

The call from Doctor Cook did eventually come. With it the somber news that yes, my father had cancer and had just been admitted to hospital. It was pretty bad; I should make plans to come and see him as soon as I could. My heart dropped. Guilt flooded through me. I had not believed my father was sick, had thought he was once again playing on my sympathies, crying wolf just one time too many.
"What shall I do?" I asked Darrell, who had come home as soon as I told him the news.
"You need to go up there and see him, Rose. I will have to stay and take care of things here at home, but I want someone with you. I know you can stay with your brother Tommy, but I would feel better if you didn't travel up there by yourself."
"I could call Suzy, see if she could come with me." I re-plied, knowing he was right. Susan, Darrell's middle daughter, and I had become quite close over the past couple of years. After calling her and explaining the situa-tion, she eagerly agreed to be my travelling companion. We would head up to Vancouver together. Before I knew it, we

were on our way north.

My visit to see my father in Vancouver turned out to be not quite what I had expected. When speaking to Doctor Cook, I had been led to believe my father was on his last legs, death was imminent; if I did not get there within a few days I would be too late. This had put me in a panic! I may have had strained relations with my father in the past, but he was still my father, my daddy. A feeling of dread filled me as I headed up to his room after Tommy dropped me off at the hospital. Suzy did not come up with me but waited patiently with Tommy. Walking into my father's room, I felt shocked. He was laying in bed, hooked up to numerous monitors, IV lines in both arms, an oxygen cannula in his nose, looking pale and fragile. My heart broke. What sort of daughter was I? How could I have not believed!

"Oh Daddy, I am here now." I said, taking his hand gently in mine, the tears flowed.

"Rose?" his voice was weak, "I knew you would come." Later that evening, after promising I would be back the following morning, all I could do was berate myself at what a terrible daughter I had been over the past few years. It was as if all my faults were laid bare before me.

The following morning, bright and early, I was once again heading up to my father's room in the hospital. As I walked down the corridor, I saw Doctor Cook and my heart fell.

"Doctor Cook! Is my father alright? Has something happened?" I asked, hurrying up to him.

"Rose, your father is fine! In fact, quite astonishing!" he reassured me with a smile.

"What do you mean?" I asked, feeling relived yet puzzled.

"We have never seen anything like it. Last night he made a turn for the better, sitting up in bed, asking for tea and something to eat. It really is extraordinary!" As we walked the remaining distance together to my father's room, my heart one minute felt elated then an uneasy feeling of trepidation seeped in. Standing beside Doctor Cook at the doorway I looked across to where yesterday my father had lain in his bed, seemingly on death's door, his breathing laboured and his features sunken into a cadaverous grey. Now the sight that greeted me was totally different. Sitting upright in bed, all tubes, monitors and IV lines removed from his body, my father saw me, and a smile lit up his face, a face which already looked healthier.

Walking to his bedside, I felt his arms embrace me as his lips brushed my cheek. Pulling up a chair by his bed I sat there, my mind in a turmoil.

"Daddy, how are you feeling today?" I asked.

His hand tightened on mine as he replied, "Better. Much better now you are here. I knew you would come! Is Darrell with you?"

"No, he had to stay at home to look after things. His daughter Susan came up with me. I just felt I had to get here as quickly as I could. You looked so poorly last night! It scared me!" I could feel the tears starting to well in my eyes.

"Well, you are here now. That's all that matters."

For the next couple of days, I sat beside him, watching as he ate robust breakfasts of sausage and eggs. Numerous times a day, he would have me head down to the nurse's station, requesting, of all things, a bowl of custard! As we talked – well as he talked – that feeling of foreboding slowly stole back over me.

"Did you get the adverts of the farms I sent you?" he asked, dipping a chocolate biscuit in his tea and glancing at me.

"Yes, daddy I did. But I already have a farm. In Oregon."

"But I could buy you a better one! Now that you are here, I am feeling so much better. We can be out of here in a day or two and go look at them. You can pick what you like. We can live wherever you want. I have already told my friend he can sell my house."

"But daddy, I'm married. I live in Oregon with Darrell. He is my life now. I can't just leave him and move back to B.C.!" Was I really understanding him correctly? He wanted to buy me a farm that we would live on together, just him and me?

"Of course you can! I can give you so much more than him. You can have horses, cows, anything you want. We can be together; you can take care of me. Of course you can leave him!" I could see a flash of anger in his eyes, hear it in his voice. My heart started pounding, I was a little girl again, knowing I was in trouble, fearful of what was coming. Then, something abruptly changed in me. I was no longer Rose Forster, I was Rose Howe, a strong, independent woman. A woman who had a husband waiting at home for her who loved her deeply.

"No daddy, I can't leave Darrell. I love him and he loves me. My life is with him. In fact, now you are so much better I am going to have to head back home. We will get things organized there and then Darrell and I can pop back up to see you." I stood up, determined to leave. I could not stay in that room anymore. I had to get out, to get away.

"Well, if you have to go you have to go. Just don't expect me to be alive when you get back!" His voice cut through me, the anger and venom in his words almost palpable. "That is if you ever come back!" he spat at me. The old Tom Forster was back in form! Guilt flooded through me as I turned and walked away.

Leaving my father like that was hard, yet all I wanted to do was get home and feel Darrell's arms around me, comforting me, telling me I had done the right thing. I was afraid. Had my father just been pretending to be so sick? He had done that in the past, numerous times. How could some-one turn around so quickly that it even amazed their own doctors? I could never, ever leave Darrell and go back to living with my father! Never! Yet the guilt was there, slowly, insidiously worming its way into my heart.

Shortly after returning home to Darrell, I received a call from Doctor Cook, telling me my father had once again taken a turn for the worse and that I needed to get up there as soon as possible. I assured him Darrell and I would drive up the following day, to please tell my father we were coming. That however was not to be. Abruptly woken a little after midnight by the strident ringing of the telephone, it was Doctor Cook calling from the hospital. My father had just passed away. I was too late. His death continued to haunt me for a very, very long time after-wards. Nightmares plagued me on a regular basis each year as the anniversary of his death approached. My father did indeed get in the last word.

Chapter 27.

Time has a way of passing all too quickly. Is there really ever enough Time? Enough days in the week or months in the year to get everything done one would wish? Time to savour precious time with the one you love. No, there is never enough time.

The next few years would see many things change in our lives, thankfully almost all for the better. Darrell continued to work hard over in Bend, making the money which allowed us to build up our farm business here in the John Day country. We eventually came to realize our expanding cow herd, horses and pigs would soon require us to have more ground than our 60 acres on the river. We really had no firm thoughts of selling and moving, it was just a tantalizing contemplation that flitted through our minds on occasion. Unfortunately, we had no hope of adding additional acreage to our river farm as Government land lay behind us and we were otherwise surrounded by the Hill's ranch, and they were not inclined to sell off any of their holdings. So, we were stuck with what we had.

One day, quite out of the blue, a local real estate chap came by our farm and started talking to Darrell. He gave us a spiel about having someone interested in buying property on the river and they just might be interested in our place, if we had ever thought of selling!

"Yes, right!" Darrell told him sardonically, not believing him at all, thinking he was just another agent looking for a listing. "If you really have someone interested, bring them by. Then we will talk." He said, fully thinking we would never see hide nor hair of the realtor again.

To our surprise, a few weeks later here comes the fellow with a lady and gentleman from neighbouring Washington state. They owned a very big alfalfa farm up there and had decided it was time to retire to a smaller place, a place such as ours! They looked around and obviously liked what they saw, for the very next day they appeared on our doorstep, asking what price we wanted for our farm. We were flabbergasted! Not even knowing ahead of time what we would ask, for we had not seriously considered selling the place, we came up with a figure and without batting an eye they said they would take it!

Now what on earth were we going to do? Unbeknownst to us, land prices had just taken a huge jump upwards and farms in our area suddenly doubled in price! Thankfully, the buyers did not want to move to Oregon right away which gave us the opportunity to lease back the farm for about a year. This gave us a little bit of time to find another home in the part of Oregon we had come to love.

Scouring the area for new land, we soon found ourselves discouraged. There were places we would have loved to have bought, but they were way out of our price range and, being the type of folks we are, the thought of going into debt by taking out a huge bank loan was not in the cards. Just when we started feeling we had made a huge blunder by selling our river farm, Fate once again showed us she had things well in hand.

After going for a drive up some of the rugged forest roads north of the village of Monument, taking a very well need-ed break from looking at properties, we were heading home when a small, weathered "For Sale" sign caught our eye. An old, abandoned schoolhouse sat at the entrance to what one could, I guess, consider a driveway, although it looked more like a dirt track through an overgrown field of dry grass and weeds. We took down the agent's telephone number and hurried home to make a call.

This was to be a turning point in our lives. The land, 414 acres to be exact, was indeed still for sale. The people who owned it were not locals. They had planned to retire and eventually build their dream home on the land, but poor health changed those plans and they had been trying to sell the acreage for quite a while. There were no buildings – other than the old schoolhouse which was definitely not livable – no improvements at all and the greater part of the property was not even fenced! The fences that were there, other than one side which adjoined a large ranch, were in a sorry state of disrepair. It was dry, bare land. No water other than a natural spring here and there and a very small creek that ran through the far side of the property. No home, no irrigation, nothing! Yet it called to us! We haggled over the price and finally a deal was made, and the land was ours.

For a while, it seemed as if our dream of staying in this part of Oregon was surely coming to an end. The way ahead uncertain. Together we made our way towards what was nothing more than another bend in the road. As we stood by the old schoolhouse looking out over the fields towards the trees in the distance, Darrell reached for my hand. Fate had opened up new horizons and opportunities for us. It would be a lot of hard work; many sacrifices would have to be made, but we were up for the challenge. We were home.

In Conclusion.

The following years have been filled with hard work, challenges, heartaches and triumphs. The day-to-day stories of
our life here on our land up Top Road could fill an entire
book! Darrell continued to work over in Bend, making a
living which allowed us build and improve the farm which
has been our home for the past 26 years. His hard work
and dedication to fulfilling our dreams took a lot of sacrifice on both our parts, yet it was worth it.

From living in a camp trailer for over a year while we built
our barn – in which we lived for five years while we built
our log home – to building a shop, butcher shop, arenas,
pig houses and numerous other improvements, hard work
has turned once bare land into the Triple H Ranch.

Along the way we have fought wildfires that threatened our
home and animals, survived health challenges that gave us
a new appreciation of life, raised cows, colts, piglets and
puppies. Held horse riding clinics for folk from all over the
country. Opened our doors to people from the city, giving
them a glance into life on a farm. I still tend to my milk
cows, making our own cheese, butter and other delicious
dairy goods. I began volunteering with our local village
ambulance. I still do as a matter of fact, becoming an EMT
instructor and teaching many classes over the years.

Darrell finally retired from his electrical contracting business and works hard on the farm side by side with me.
Each year he raises a magnificent vegetable garden while
still finding time to restore old cars – a passion of his!

Through all the trials and tribulations over the years, one
thing remains firm above all: our love for each other. We
are best pals. Fate led us to each other. Fate encouraged

me to keep walking even when the road was rocky and hard, Fate brought me to the bend in the road and gave me the courage to peek around the corner. Will there be other bends in the road? Maybe, but hand in hand with my dearest Darrell we will gladly walk forward to meet them.

This is not The End, for the Journey through life will always Continue...

BEND IN THE ROAD

Made in the USA
Monee, IL
22 January 2022

88867347R00132